THE LIVING ROOM SERIES

FINDING GOD FAITHFUL

A STUDY ON
THE LIFE OF JOSEPH

KELLY MINTER

Lifeway Press® Brentwood, Tennessee

Published by Lifeway Press® • © 2023 Kelly Minter

ISBN: 978-1-4300-8700-7
Item: 005846301
Dewey decimal classification: 234.2
Subject heading: JOSEPH, SON OF JACOB / FAITH / PROVIDENCE AND
           GOVERNMENT OF GOD

To order additional copies of this resource, write Lifeway Church Resources Customer Service; 200 Powell Place, Suite 100; Brentwood, TN 37027-7707; FAX order to 615.251.5933; call toll-free 800.458.2772; email orderentry@lifeway.com.

Printed in the United States of America

Adult Ministry Publishing, Lifeway Church Resources, 200 Powell Place, Suite 100 Brentwood, TN 37027-7707

EDITORIAL TEAM, ADULT MINISTRY PUBLISHING

Faith Whatley
Director, Adult Ministry

Michelle Hicks
Manager, Adult Ministr
Short Term Bible Studie

Mike Wakefield
Content Editor

Sarah Doss
Production Editor

Lauren Ervin
Art Director

Bekah Wertz
Graphic Designer

Chelsea Waack
Graphic Designer

TABLE OF CONTENTS

MEET THE AUTHOR
KELLY MINTER

Kelly Minter is passionate about teaching the Bible, and she believes it permeates all of life. She's found personal healing and steadfast hope in the pages of Scripture. When she's not singing, writing, or speaking, you can find her picking homegrown vegetables, enjoying her six nieces and nephews, or riding a boat down the Amazon River with Justice & Mercy International. A Southern transplant, Kelly delights in neighborhood walks, watching college football, and a diner mug of good coffee with her closest friends.

Kelly's love for the Word of God led her to create Cultivate, an event centered around Scripture, worship, prayer, and missions. This gospel-centered, approachable event invites women of all ages to dig deeply into God's Word and encounter Him afresh.

Kelly's love for the Word of God also led her to write in-depth Bible studies like the one you hold in your hands. Those Bible studies include, *Ruth: Loss, Love & Legacy*; *Nehemiah: A Heart That Can Break* ; *What Love Is: The Letters of 1, 2, 3 John*; *All Things New: A Study on 2 Corinthians*; and *No Other Gods: The Unrivaled Pursuit of Christ*. Kelly's music includes *Hymns & Hallelujahs*, which accompanies her *All Things New* Bible study.

Wherever the River Runs: How a Forgotten People Renewed My Hope in the Gospel is Kelly's first memoir about her life-changing journeys to the Amazon jungle with Justice & Mercy International (JMI). Kelly partners with JMI, an organization that cares for the vulnerable and forgotten in the Amazon and Moldova. To view more about Kelly's studies, books, music, and Cultivate events, visit www.kellyminter.com.

INTRODUCTION

Joseph's story welcomes us with open arms, summons us into the living room, and invites us to sit down awhile and listen. So many have found a dear companion in Joseph because his life displays much of the human experience. We all "get" Joseph on some level. We can relate to him. We've probably never owned a multicolored robe that nearly cost us our lives or traveled as a slave by camel to a foreign land, but we patently understand difficult family relationships. We've experienced betrayal. We know unfair. Broken dreams have nearly sunk us. And almost every one of us has wondered at some point in our lives, *Where is God?*

Joseph's story doesn't necessarily answer all of our questions, but biblical stories rarely do. They actually accomplish something more important. Biblical stories reveal truths about God, our world, and ourselves, and in doing so, they sweep us into the much bigger story that's being told: the saving story of Jesus. In *Finding God Faithful* we'll discover that as epic and important as Joseph's account is, it's actually but a tiny act in God's grand narrative of redemption, The Story. While we study Joseph's story, we will pay best attention to God's.

So what does all of this mean for us? For the stay-at-home mom, the business owner, the newly married, or the single mom trying to make her way in the world in the twenty-first century? Well, I'm glad you asked. Genesis 37–50 (Joseph's account) reveals how deeply God loves us and wants us to love others—even those most difficult to love. (No matter who in your life is a challenging personality, just wait until you meet Joseph's brothers. They'll make your irritable Aunt Jane look like she's up for this year's Nobel Peace Prize.) On a very practical level, Joseph's life will encourage us to run for our lives from temptation, to serve when we're suffering, and to serve when we're prospering. And if you've ever wondered when to protect yourself from the people who have wounded you or when to lay down your defenses, throw your arms around your foes, and weep, Joseph's story can help. It doesn't give us a manual, but boy does it offer us an epic scene.

This is to say nothing of what Joseph's story teaches us about how God can take the stones thrown at us with evil intent and use them as the bedrock of His good plans for our lives. No one will ever describe the mystery quite like Joseph; "You planned evil against me; God planned it for good … " (Gen. 50:20). Which brings us to another quite practical theme of Joseph's story: forgiveness. If Joseph could forgive his brothers, I imagine there's no one we can't learn to forgive.

For those of you who have ever wondered if your dark nights and crushing heartbreak were sure signs that God had forgotten or abandoned you, Joseph's story confidently tells us otherwise. In a faraway land, and later in a dismal prison, what more hopeful truth could be written than "God was with Joseph"? Whether in prison or in palace, His presence changes everything. Perhaps above all, in this study, I hope you will gather a richer understanding of God's promises, His faithfulness to His people, and the person of Jesus toward whom Joseph's entire story is aimed.

SET APART

GROUP DISCUSSION

What portion of the video teaching really resonated with you? Why?

God didn't give Abraham many details when He called him out of Haran. How does Abraham's act of faith help you trust in the God of the destination over the destination itself?

How do you think Abraham's intimacy with God deepened as he followed God's leading?

What does it mean to be set apart from the world, to be a blessing to the world (Gen. 12:1-3)?

We're often tempted to take charge of the tasks God has called us to instead of depending on His leadership. How can we actively follow God in obedience yet trust Him for the outcome?

Abraham obeyed God's leading. How have you seen God accomplish His purposes through your obedience? (Especially when you would have done things differently.)

Joseph was born into a complicated family, but that didn't keep God from setting him apart for a great purpose. How has God set you apart to follow Him despite your past or heritage?

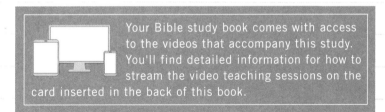

Your Bible study book comes with access to the videos that accompany this study. You'll find detailed information for how to stream the video teaching sessions on the card inserted in the back of this book.

THE UNLIKELY PATH OF BLESSING

My best friend and I sat on the front stoop of my parents' old house where we talked about our future plans and dreams. I was in college at the time, and she had recently graduated. I'd grown up in an intact family, while both her parents had had multiple marriages. "The bus is stopping here and I'm getting off," my friend asserted. I was well acquainted with her story and knew exactly what she meant. Despite having come from a line of indiscretions and broken marriages, she was determined to live a different life. She was hopping off the generational bus that had continually run the same sordid line, choosing to be led by Christ and not defined by her family's past.

It's been at least twenty years since that conversation on the stoop. I've never forgotten her line about getting off the bus—time has a way of proving which bus we're actually on. All these years later, she'd confidently tell you that, by the grace of God, Jesus has defined her life apart from the generational and familial patterns that often feel as inescapable as our DNA. If I didn't believe Jesus could do this, what we're about to study in Joseph's life would simply be an anomaly instead of a testimony to what God is still doing today—bringing beauty from ashes.

As we begin our study of Joseph's life, we're going to see a life that, given the circumstances, shouldn't have made it out of the teenage years, much less flourished. Without giving too many of the details away, Joseph was born into a family pierced by jealousy, favoritism, and competition—even murderous rage. His family of origin hardly set him up for success, spiritual or otherwise. On top of that, the tragic turn his life took as a young man certainly seemed irredeemable. Joseph's emergence as a humble leader who would save a nation can only be explained by the power of God to triumph over the power of our pasts.

As we begin our first week of personal study, I want to encourage you: Your identity need not stay rooted in past failures or past sin, even a past or harmful environment you had no control over. When you surrender to Jesus, the old and frail no longer have sway over the redemptive work He promises to do in your life. If God took what was meant for evil in Joseph's life and used it for good, will He not do the same for you?

DAY 1
SETTING THE STAGE

GENESIS 12:1-9

My grandfather, Charles S. Minter Jr., was an admiral in the Navy and the superintendent of the United States Naval Academy from 1964–1965. Since his death in 2008, our family has been enamored with any new bits of information about his life that turn up. My brother recently found a transcript of an interview my grandfather did in the '80s. In that transcript we found pieces of news even my father didn't know, like the fact that my grandfather's grandfather was a Presbyterian minister in Covington, Virginia.

In light of this discovery, I couldn't help but wonder if my great, great grandfather and his wife ever specifically prayed for the generations that would follow them. Did they ask God for their descendants to love Him, His Word, and His people? Is the work my Dad has been doing as a pastor for more than forty years and the work I'm doing now something seeded in us by God through the prayers of people we've never met? Of course God is always at work before any of us arrive on the scene, but it's been interesting to consider the ways He might have been working before me in my ancestors.

Joseph's story will be far more meaningful to us once we understand how God moved in the people before Joseph.

Similarly, I believe understanding Joseph's story will be far more meaningful to us once we understand how God moved in the people before Joseph. When I say *similarly*, I mean in principle only; God did something unparalleled in the life of Joseph's great grandfather Abraham that would not only change Joseph's life but would change the world forever. We'll trace some of those happenings so we can best appreciate what God was doing in the lives of Joseph, his brothers, all of Israel, and eventually you and me. But not all today—sorry, if I just stressed you out, because I just got a little overwhelmed myself.

LET'S BEGIN OUR STUDY BY READING GENESIS 11:31–12:9.

According to 11:31, where was Abraham living when God called him to leave? (Note: God would later change Abram's name to Abraham in Genesis 17:5, so I'll refer to him as the latter.)

Pulling your answer only from 12:1, to what land did God call Abraham to go? away from your country

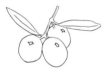

PERSONAL TAKE: Try to imagine being in Abraham's position. How would God's vague instructions about your future destination be difficult for you?

I will bless those who bless you, I will curse anyone who treats you with contempt, and all the peoples on earth shall be blessed through you.

Genesis 12:3

According to 12:3, who specifically would be blessed through Abraham as a result of his obedience to God's leading? all families who bless you

God's covenant with Abraham is the bedrock of our study, so we're going to commit to memory three promises God made to Abraham:

1. **Land:** God promised Abraham and his people the promised land of Canaan.
2. **Descendants:** God promised to multiply Abraham's descendants, making nations come from him.
3. **Blessing:** God promised to bless Abraham and to bless all the peoples of the world through Abraham.

By majestic grace, God pulled Abraham from his father's family, a family that served other gods (Josh. 24:2), and told Abraham He would bless him, multiply his family, and make him into a blessing for the whole world. And there began the beginning of Israel's history.

Note: Joseph was born only two generations after God's covenant with Abraham. Hold onto this significant information.

READ GALATIANS 3:7-9.

In verse 8, the apostle Paul quoted from Genesis 12:3. As part of God's promise to Abraham that all nations would be blessed, who has God justified? Gentiles

What is required to be blessed through Abraham? Paul uses the word four times in these verses. (Circle the best answer below.)

Belief   Righteousness   (Faith)   Passion

We're left with a question that begs to be asked, *Faith in what?* The prevailing thought of our day is to have faith in yourself and believe that you're enough. I know myself too well to feel good about this premise. We see another widely accepted option in our current culture: put your faith in a variety of things—certain religions, regular trips to the yoga studio, healthy eating, or the general good of humanity. The apostle Paul helps us narrow this down.

CONTINUE READING GALATIANS 3; LET'S MOVE TO VERSES 13-14.

Who redeemed us and therefore is the only one worthy of our faith?

Jesus

What did Jesus redeem us from?

curse of the law

What did we receive as part of God's promise to Abraham?

Spirit

The connections Paul makes between God's covenant with Abraham and Jesus' redemption of the Gentiles will continue to crystalize throughout our study. In the meantime, I simply want you to see that there are connections. You and I are part of the fulfillment of the promise God made to Abraham all those thousands of years ago in the desert of Haran, a promise He later affirmed in the land of Canaan. As we study the life of Joseph, we'll watch this promise unfold, following it all the way to our modern-day lives and beyond.

Since God's call to Abraham affected all of humanity, tracing his family line to the arrival of Joseph will give us further insight into Joseph's story and our own. If you're thinking this activity will be fairly straightforward, keep in mind these were not the days of a single-spouse marriage with two kids and a white picket fence. Family lines in the ancient Near East usually included at least a couple of wives for every man, a few maidservants, and multitudes of half-siblings among the children. And their figurative white picket fence encompassed the entire land of Canaan, a boundary line half the descendants didn't pay attention to anyhow.

Intrigued? Here we go.

READ GENESIS 17:15-19.

Ishmael was the son of Abraham and Hagar, Sarah's maidservant; Isaac was the son of Abraham and Sarah. Through which son would God's covenant with Abraham continue? (Circle the correct answer.)

Ishmael   Isaac

READ GENESIS 25:19-20,24-26.

What are the names of the twins born to Isaac and his wife, Rebekah?

Jacob, Esau

READ GENESIS 25:22-23 AND 28:1-4.

With which of Rebekah and Isaac's sons did God confirm His covenant? (Circle the correct answer.)

(Jacob)   Esau

READ GENESIS 29:21-28.

What two women did Jacob marry?

Leah   Rachael

So far we've learned that God made a covenant with Abraham.
God then confirmed that covenant through Abraham and Sarah's son,
Isaac. He continued to confirm it through Isaac and
Rebekah's son Jacob.

We're now circling in on the central figure of our story: Joseph.

READ GENESIS 30:22-24.

Continue filling out the family tree. Joseph's father was Jacob
and his mother was Rachael.

You've pieced a lot of genealogical information together today. Well done! If you feel like all you've done today is list the names of some abstract people, let me assure you more family chaos and relational mayhem are attached to these people than you and I have ever seen. You'll really enjoy tomorrow's drama—if you like that sort of thing, of course.

As we close our first day together I want to return to where we began—Genesis 12:1. God told Abraham, I want you to leave your land, your relatives, your father's house, and go to the place I will show you. This verse perfectly sums up our faith journey, doesn't it? At some point in our walks with Christ we have to let go of what we think we know is best and take hold of what He says is best. We have to forsake what feels so natural, and what we've grown accustomed to, for what He promises will give us life. God doesn't often give us a clear picture of the places we're going, only a clear picture of Himself so we can follow Him there.

At some point in our walks with Christ we have to let go of what we think we know is best and take hold of what He says is best.

PERSONAL RESPONSE: How does Abraham's faith to follow God into the unknown challenge and encourage you? Take some time with this.

To trust, have faith God will lead us

READ 2 CORINTHIANS 5:7.

By what means do we walk with God?

faith

READ HEBREWS 10:23.

What encourages and inspires us to hold onto the hope we have in Jesus?

He is faithful

While Abraham's faith is inspiring, I'm grateful God's covenant plan didn't rest on a human's faith but on God's own promises, which are secured in His character. I'm also thankful that those promises would prevail despite the human frailty, selfishness, and division that will characterize some of Abraham's descendants.

In closing, go to page 18 and fill in the family tree with the names you read about today. I hope this exercise will help you continue to piece together God's covenant through Abraham's family, particularly the role Joseph will play. (For a succinct list of names, go to Gen. 35:23-26.)

JACOB'S FAMILY TREE

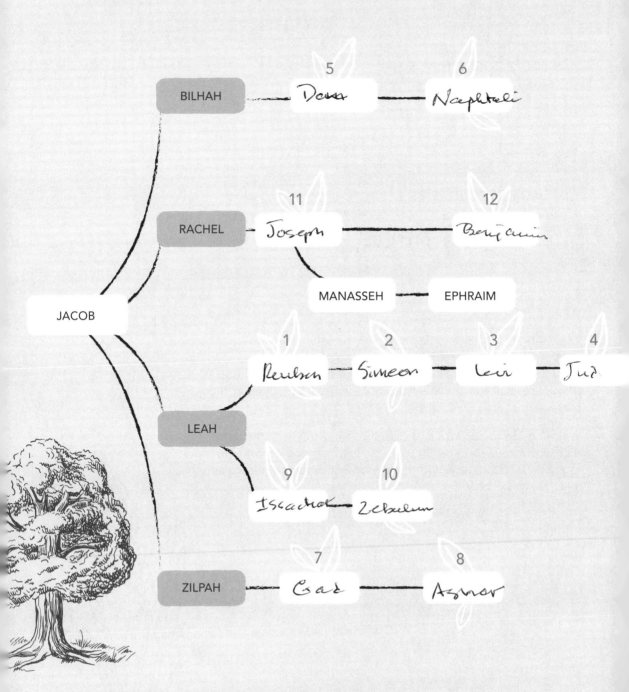

DAY 2
BORN INTO DRAMA
GENESIS 29:16–30:24

Anyone who's read books on psychology or been through counseling is familiar with the ways our families of origin affect our development and who we become. Thankfully, our families of origin don't have to dictate the trajectories of our lives—especially with the indwelling of the Holy Spirit, who has the power to renew us and break through generational patterns of unhealthy and destructive behavior (2 Cor. 10:3-4). Exploring the family Joseph was born into will give us a clearer picture of who he was and the struggles he faced. Today is going to be fun, if for no other reason than we'll be dealing with someone else's drama instead of our own, which is always more enjoyable for me.

Thankfully, our families of origin don't have to dictate the trajectories of our lives.

READ GENESIS 29:16-30. YOU COVERED SOME OF THIS PASSAGE YESTERDAY, BUT READ IT AGAIN IN VIEW OF LEAH'S PLIGHT.

PERSONAL TAKE: In what ways did Laban set up Leah for heartache and rejection? How might this have affected her overall well-being as a wife and mother?

READ GENESIS 29:31–30:24. I KNOW THIS TEXT IS A BIT LONGER, BUT IT PROVIDES HELPFUL CONTEXT AND WILL SETTLE YOU INTO THE STORY.

What did Rachel have that Leah desperately wanted? What did Leah have that Rachel desperately wanted?

love, children

What did Leah hope having children would do for her relationship with Jacob? List every hope. (See Gen. 29:32; 29:34; 30:20.)

love, be attached, dwell with her

Even though Jacob chose Rachel as the love of his life, describe her overall state in Genesis 30:1.

distraught

How did Rachel try to "fix" her problem of not being able to bear children?

gave Jacob her maid

Then God remembered Rachel.

Genesis 30:22a

PERSONAL TAKE: How would the angst, jealousy, and longing in both of Jacob's marriages have affected the environment the children grew up in? What kind of effect would it have had on the children's relationships with one another? jealousy

Remember, we began our study by looking at God's covenant with Abraham—to bless his family and bring a great nation from him. So far things aren't looking as promising as I would have hoped.

PERSONAL REFLECTION: Are you currently hanging on to one of God's promises in the midst of what feels like a complicated disaster? Or maybe you're hanging on to His presence in a state of unfulfilled longing? If so, how does today's passage encourage you, in light of the fact that God used this broken family to fulfill His promises?

LOOK BACK AT GENESIS 30:22-24.

What did Rachel say had been taken away from her when Joseph was born? her reproach

The Hebrew word used here for disgrace (or reproach) is *herpâ*, and it means a "state of dishonor and low status."[1] In ancient Hebrew culture, a woman's worth was bound up in her family. Her legacy was based on her ability to bear children, especially sons, who would carry on the family name.

PERSONAL REFLECTION: Given this cultural insight and everything else you've read today, describe how Rachel might have felt when she held Joseph in her arms, knowing that God Himself had reached down and taken away her disgrace.

Remembered is another important word in verse 22, "Then God *remembered* Rachel" (*emphasis mine*). First, "when the Lord 'remembers' in Genesis and Exodus, this activity is often tied to God's covenant with Israel."[2] And by using the word, *remembered*, the narrator is signaling to us that God's upcoming work in Rachel's life is significant to His covenant with Abraham and the future nation of Israel. Rachel is part of a grander story.

The word *remember* in the Old Testament also indicates God's action. This might be confusing for us because our modern usage of *remember* gives the impression that for all these years God had forgotten Rachel. It sounds almost as if after having divinely arranged Rachel and Jacob's meeting and after a lovely wedding reception, God plumb forgot to put her pregnancy on His calendar. Fortunately, this is not what the word means here at all. Robert D. Bergen says it this way, "'Remembered' is a soteriological verb when used with the Lord as the subject and *suggests the initiation of a major new activity by the covenant-making God"* (*emphasis mine*).[3]

Soteriological: (adj.) dealing with the doctrine of salvation

God's remembering us will never be separated from His divine activity and His perfect timing in our lives. While Rachel was waiting on the Lord for a child, He was preparing to give her a son who would have a profound effect on the future of God's chosen people. Though Rachel had prayed for many years, seemingly to no avail, God heard her prayers and had a far greater plan than she could have imagined.

PERSONAL RESPONSE: What are you waiting on the Lord for? How does Rachel's experience encourage you to hope in God's divine activity in your circumstances as you pray and seek Him?

While it's good to wait on God for the things we long for, how we wait on Him is just as important. In your waiting, tell the Lord you trust His timing and believe in His power to achieve your heart's desire. Surrender your agenda to Him. And where your faith lacks, pray these words from Mark 9:24, "I do believe; help my unbelief!"

Grace showed up anyway in the arms of a broken woman named Rachel, in the form of a baby boy named Joseph, by the power of Yahweh, the God of Israel.

Today we welcomed our study's main character, Joseph, into the world. We learned that his birth was a profound joy to Rachel and that through it Almighty God had taken away her disgrace. We also discovered that Joseph's birth came about because God keeps His promises. He was faithful to remember Rachel because He remembered His covenant with Abraham that all the nations of the earth would be blessed through his family. (Of course, at Joseph's birth, no one could have imagined Joseph would accomplish that blessing from a position of power in Egypt.)

God acted at just the right time. Abraham's descendants were a bit of a mess, yes, but grace showed up anyway in the arms of a broken woman named Rachel, in the form of a baby boy named Joseph, by the power of Yahweh, the God of Israel.

DAY 3
FAVORITISM AND JEALOUSY

GENESIS 37:1-11

Today we step onto the soil where Joseph grew up. We find him as a seventeen-year-old tending sheep with his brothers in the midst of complex family dynamics, many of which stemmed from the favoritism of his father and the jealousy of his brothers. If you'd hoped we could ease into Joseph's story with a cup of chamomile and a "once upon a time" opening line, the author of Genesis gives us no such luxury. Instead he takes the more direct approach of immediately plunging us into the middle of a dysfunctional family. If you need that cup of tea, you'll have to pour it yourself or come over to my house.

If nothing else, many of us will find these pages of Genesis relatable. Despite the cultural differences of wardrobe choice, empty cisterns, and bizarre dreams involving bowing sheaves, the longings of the human heart appear to have stayed the same. Thankfully, the God who transforms our hearts hasn't changed either. And with that hopeful reminder, we'll begin our story.

READ GENESIS 37:1-11.

Write down anything that stands out to you from these verses and explain why it stands out. Joseph must have known telling his brothers this dream it would infuriate them

Compare Genesis 37:3 with Genesis 25:27-28 and 29:30. What problematic similarities do you see in these passages?

Look back at Genesis 33:1-3. What generational seed planted by Isaac and Rebekah showed up in Jacob's marriage and parenting?

Favoritism

As we address the deeper issues of favoritism and jealousy that fractured Jacob's family, my prayer is for God to bring healing to our relationships that may be broken in similar ways and for similar reasons.

PERSONAL REFLECTION: If favoritism has affected your family of origin, current family, friendships, or work relationships, describe its effects below.

When we show favoritism to someone, we don't do so in isolation.

Knowing the difference between favoritism and a special love or fondness for someone can be difficult. Doing something for someone based on what I'll receive in return can be an indicator of unhealthy favoritism, as is doing something for someone out of fear of losing them. Perhaps the simplest way of putting it is this: While love and friendship are based on selflessness, favoritism is typically based on selfishness.

TURN TO THE NEW TESTAMENT, AND READ JAMES 2:1-9. (HOLD YOUR PLACE IN JAMES. WE'LL BE BACK THERE AT THE END OF TODAY'S STUDY.)

Why did the person in this example show favoritism to the one and not the other?

Why does James specifically say we shouldn't show favoritism?

When we show favoritism to someone, we don't do so in isolation; others in our lives are affected. In the James passage, because the rich person was favored, the poor person was obviously shamed. Likewise, in Genesis, Joseph's brothers were hurt by Jacob's favoritism of him.

List the strong words of animosity used to describe the brothers' feelings toward Joseph. (See Gen. 37:4-5,8,11.)

hate, envy

I've often wondered why Joseph shared his dreams with his brothers. Did he do it out of excitement or spite? Did he hope they might start showing him respect? We're not told Joseph's motives in the biblical narrative, but the effects of his confession on the brothers are obvious. I'm reminded here of the importance of pure motives and wise timing when we talk about the good and exciting things in our lives—even the things *God* is doing. While we can't *make* others jealous, we don't want to unwisely foster it.

PERSONAL REFLECTION: In our age of social media, how can you be thoughtful about what you choose to share and not share based on today's passages?

Because of Joseph's dreams and Jacob's partiality toward Joseph, the brothers allowed jealousy to overtake their hearts and determine their decisions. *The Dictionary of Biblical Languages* defines of *jealousy* as, "having a feeling of ill will ranging even to anger, based on a perceived advantage, or a desire for exclusivity in relationship."[4]

PERSONAL TAKE: Define *jealousy* in your own words. *Someone having something you want for yourself*

I think of jealousy as being consumed with resentment toward someone because he or she has what I think I need for life and happiness.

PERSONAL REFLECTION: Is there anyone you're jealous of right now? If so, write down the reason behind your jealousy.

TURN BACK TO JAMES AND READ 3:13-18.

PERSONAL REFLECTION: Why do you think jealousy (or envy) and selfish ambition produce disorder and evil practices? Take some time to think about this. *Anger, feelings of inadequacy*

James describes what happens when selfish ambitions rule our lives and relationships. But he also paints an inspiring picture of a person whose life is characterized by wisdom that's pure, gentle, and full of mercy and peace. When I'm given to jealousy I look nothing like this wise, gentle, and peaceful person.

The past couple of years I have experienced some uncanny challenges in my work. While a close friend of mine was prospering in the exact area in which I was drowning, I battled jealousy. (I don't know what jealousy looks like on you, but it looks terrible on me—worse than the time I cut my own bangs in junior high and thought wearing a pink bandanna would help. Truth.)

I had to recognize that Jesus doesn't love my friend more than He loves me just because He's given her the very thing I want, the thing I'm pretty sure I need. In my place of longing God has invited me to trust Him and His goodness. And when I'm secure in His provision, I can be

But the wisdom from above is first pure, then peace-loving, gentle, compliant, full of mercy and good fruits, unwavering, without pretense.

James 3:17

In my place of longing God has invited me to trust Him and His goodness.

happy for those around me. My character becomes marked by peace and kindness, not the worldly wisdom of envying others and tirelessly grasping for what I want.

Today we leave Joseph caught between the crushing boulders of his father's favoritism and his brothers' jealousy. The removal of either of these obstacles would have helped restore peace to a fractured family. So that's what I want you to think about today. How can you remove partiality and jealousy from your life? It just might be the change that saves some of your most precious relationships.

PERSONAL RESPONSE: Is there someone to whom you're showing favoritism based on selfishness or your desire to control? Not only does this hurt the person you're favoring, the way it hurt Joseph, but it also hurts those in the vicinity, the way it hurt Joseph's brothers. Confess this to the Lord and ask Him for Christlike love to replace partiality.

PERSONAL RESPONSE: Are you jealous of someone? Confess your jealousy to the Lord. Confess to Him whatever it is this person has that you desperately want. Ask God to meet that need in you however He desires. He is good and delights to give good gifts to you (Matt. 7:9-11).

The beauty of Joseph's story is that in the midst of favoritism, jealousy, and anger, God is working out His purposes. His covenant promises will prevail despite the sin and brokenness of the people to whom the promises were made. God is faithful. This story would have been much less tumultuous if everyone could have recognized at the time that while God does choose different people for different things, He is altogether good and doesn't show favoritism (Acts 10:34; Rom. 2:11). I wish Jacob and the brothers could have known that Joseph's dreams would prove to be good news for them, that they were part of God's story, as well. By the end of our study together, I hope you, too, will be convinced of this.

If you still need that cup of tea, my kettle is on for you.

DAY 4
WHEN WE DON'T UNDERSTAND

GENESIS 37:12-28

As you read today's passage be on the lookout for God's providential hand throughout the narrative. It's easy for us to think of God as being "way up there" in the heavens on His end of the universe while we plod along in our daily lives with little intervention from Him. But here in Genesis, long before the incarnation of Jesus, we see God at work on earth. We see Him moving in specific locations on the map, guiding people, orchestrating events, and working out His covenant promises.

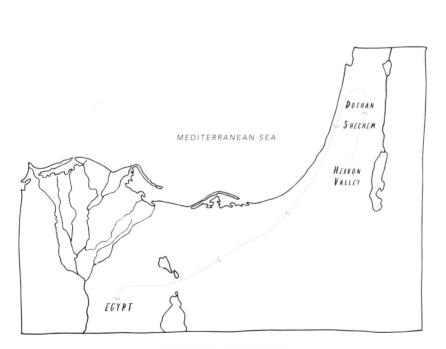

JOSEPH'S JOURNEY

From memory, God's covenant with Abraham consisted of what three promises? (See Day 1 of this week on p. 14 if you need help.)

1. land
2. many ancestors/decendents
3. bless all people thru Abraham

READ GENESIS 37:12-28.

Little did Jacob know when he sent his beloved son Joseph on a journey to find his brothers, Jacob wouldn't see Joseph again for more than twenty years. And he would never again see Joseph in the land of Canaan.

Joseph searched for his brothers by traveling north from the Hebron Valley to a place called Shechem. According to Genesis 12:6-7, what significant event took place in Shechem?

Abraham passed thru on way to Canaan

Who do you think is the unnamed man in Genesis 37:15-17?

Angel

They said to one another, "Oh, look, here comes that dream expert!"

Genesis 37:19

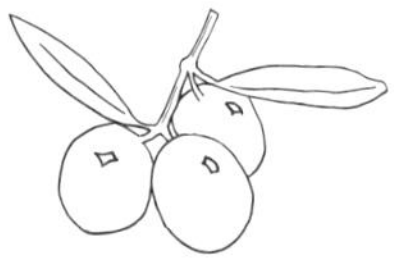

Jewish tradition views this man as an angel.[5] I don't think we can know for sure who he is, but in the words of K. A. Matthews, "Whether the 'man' is an angel or a human, the unseen hand of the Lord is apparent here.[6]

PERSONAL REFLECTION: Describe a time you've "seen" the unseen hand of the Lord in the past year?

Western Wall in Jerusalem,

PERSONAL TAKE: At just the sight of Joseph in the distance the brothers began plotting to kill him. Genesis 37:19 gives us further insight into the reason behind their hatred. What was their reason, and why do you think it bothered them to the point of wanting to murder their brother?

They would bow down to Joseph - he would rule over them

We'll come back to Genesis 37:20 at the very end of our study. But, I want you to hang onto it throughout our time together, so finish the passage below.

"So now, come on, let's kill him and throw him into one of the pits. We can say that a vicious animal ate him. Then we'll see __what will become of his dreams__ *!" (CSB).*

Out of the darkness flickered a bit of brotherly care and protection as Reuben pleaded with his brothers, urging them to throw Joseph into a dry cistern instead of killing him. We're told that Reuben suggested this plan so he could later rescue Joseph and return him to their father. Whatever Reuben's motives (he had previously angered his father so he may have wanted to use Joseph's rescue to get back in Jacob's good graces), it's a reminder to us that speaking up for what's right can have enormous impact. Maybe even save a person's life. Or thousands of lives.

The brothers' murderous plotting may be an extreme case, but the principle remains. It's easy to go along with the current of the crowd instead of risking something for the sake of an individual. It makes me think of Isaiah 58 where God talks about true fasting, "Is it not to share your bread with the hungry, to bring the poor and homeless into your house, to clothe the naked when you see him, and not to ignore your own flesh and blood?" (v. 7).

PERSONAL RESPONSE: I wonder if there's someone the Lord is asking you to protect, defend, or stand up for. It may be your child's classmate, a coworker who's being falsely accused, a family member caught in addiction, or someone else who needs help. Write that person's name below and record what you feel prompted to do on his or her behalf.

Keisha
Connie

According to Genesis 37:26, what was Judah's motive for deciding not to kill Joseph? profit and guilt/sin

Joseph was sold for twenty pieces of silver, the going rate for a healthy young man in the early second millennium. People from the land of Canaan are commonly found in Egyptian records as slaves in various roles.[7] You would think that approximately four thousand years after this horrific scene human trafficking would be wiped clean from our world. Tragically, it is still happening all over the globe, even in our own backyards. (See note at the end of today's study.)

We've covered a lot of ground in today's passage, much of it painful to digest. We'll revisit Genesis chapter 37 many times near the end of our story because we'll want to see how God was active and present even in the midst of such suffering and evil. I can't wait to look back with you and see how God—even in this situation—was taking what was meant for evil and turning it into good.

IN THE MEANTIME, TURN TO 2 CORINTHIANS 1:3-5.

How is God described in verse 3?

Father, grace, mercies, comfort

What always overflows alongside our suffering (v. 5)?

consolation

What is one of the purposes of our suffering (v. 4)?

To comfort others

My prayer is that we'll better understand both suffering and sovereignty from the perspective of God's Word, so that we'll see His hand more clearly and trust His heart more deeply. Our God is good.

After reading today's portion of Joseph's story it seems as though God has lost control. It appeared Joseph was being kicked around the landscape like a rubber ball on an elementary playground. His father sent him to Shechem, a mysterious man redirected him to Dothan, and then his brothers, after deciding not to kill him, secured him a one-way ticket to Egypt by way of Ishmaelite traders.

The story appears senseless. Reckless. Out of control. Could God's providential hand still be at work in Joseph's life? Is it possible that what appears to be nothing but a tangle of other people's agendas will somehow be the very ball of yarn God will use to weave one of the most redemptive masterpieces in human history? We won't solve the problem of why a good God allows suffering, nor will we fully understand God's sovereignty at the end of our eight weeks together. But my prayer is that we'll better understand both suffering and sovereignty from the perspective of God's Word, so that we'll see His hand more clearly and trust His heart more deeply. Our God is good.

PERSONAL RESPONSE: What stood out to you the most in today's personal study and why?

jealousy and how it affects others around us

Joseph's brothers may have been able to destroy his coat of many colors, but they would never be able to destroy the dreams God had given him. Hang on to that, dear friends.

Note: If the Lord is stirring in your heart to help fight against human trafficking, there are many organizations doing this important work. I work with Justice & Mercy International (JMI), an organization that stops trafficking in the developing Eastern European country of Moldova before it happens. To find out more, visit justiceandmercy.org.

DAY 5
GOD WAS WITH JOSEPH
GENESIS 37:29-36; 39:1-6

We can get through just about any pain or suffering if we know the Lord is in it with us. But when we feel forsaken or abandoned, our pain becomes unbearable. In a most trying circumstance, the psalmist expressed what the Lord's presence meant to him with the imagery, "Even when I go through the darkest valley, I fear no danger, for *you are with me*; your rod and your staff—they comfort me" (Ps. 23:4, *emphasis mine*). In Genesis 39, we'll see the recurring phrase, "The LORD was with Joseph." Joseph's entire story rests on these five words. They will prove to be an anchor in turbulence and reconciliation in what seems irreconcilable. In the words of Beth Moore, "Where God does not grant our request, He will grant us His comfort. No small trade indeed. He is everything."[8] And He will be everything for Joseph.

The LORD was with Joseph.

Genesis 39:2a

READ GENESIS 37:29-36.

In what ways did the brothers deceive Jacob without flatly lying to him, and why is this especially troubling? Gave him Josephs wear- kelted robe w/ blood on it

We're not sure where Reuben, the firstborn, went in between the brothers throwing Joseph into the pit and Joseph being sold to the Midianites. Reuben's absence, however, made way for Judah, the fourth born, to execute his own plan without interference. These may seem like subtle details, but Judah's influence over his brothers and his rising position will prove significant later.

Look back at verses 33-35. What was so insidious about Jacob's sons trying to comfort him?

I'm trying to picture the scene: the brothers circled around their dad speaking comforting words to him, embracing him with loud cries, knowing all the while that his son wasn't dead, rather that he'd been sold at their very hands. Based on the brothers' fabricated evidence, Jacob drew his own conclusion that Joseph had been devoured by an animal. So technically the brothers didn't lie about what really happened, perhaps relieving their own consciences, albeit falsely.

While we're quick to condemn the brothers for their deceit, how many times have we tried to comfort someone we've hurt without first admitting the pain we've inflicted upon them? How many times have we tried to make amends without first giving an honest and heartfelt confession? How many times have we knowingly led someone down the wrong path without technically lying?

I have a friend whose husband has essentially abandoned their marriage. He feels mildly guilty for walking out on his wife and for the pain he's caused her. If he were truly repentant, he would confess his sin to my friend and turn his heart back to her. Instead, he justifies his wrongdoings and tries to comfort her by buying her gifts and paying her bills. Verse 35 reminds me that there's no chance of comforting those we've wounded without first having repented.

PERSONAL RESPONSE: Have you hurt someone and instead of admitting your wrong and repenting of it, you've tried to comfort them through gifts or actions? If so, make this right before God and the other person. You'll never be free and the person you've hurt will never be able to truly receive your comfort until you do.

Chapter 38 takes a detour from the life of Joseph and follows Judah on a wild journey out of Canaan. We'll come back to this chapter in future weeks.

IN THE MEANTIME, SKIP CHAPTER 38 AND READ GENESIS 39:1-6.

Into what nation was Joseph sold and to what person?

Egypt, Potiphar

We began our study with God's call on Abraham's life and the covenant God made with him. Based on the land that God promised to give Abraham and his descendants in Genesis 12:4-7, why would arriving in Egypt have been particularly difficult for Joseph to process?

Not part of Canaan

PERSONAL REFLECTION: Have you ever found yourself in a perplexing situation in which God seemed to be working contrary to your understanding of His plan? How does this turn in Joseph's life encourage you to trust God's plans and presence?

NOW LOOK UP GENESIS 15:13-14.

How might Joseph's forced trip to Egypt be linked to this prophecy God gave Abraham? Descendents will be strangers in a land that is not theirs

Many years before Joseph's descent into Egypt God foretold that the Israelites would be enslaved in a foreign land. We don't know if Joseph was aware of this revelation, but it shows us that God's hand was on Joseph's steps even though his journey must have felt fully to the contrary. (Note: I'm not suggesting that the evil plan of the brothers or being sold into slavery were somehow good things because God's plan was being worked out. We'll later hear Joseph refer to his brothers' actions as plainly evil.) The interplay between God's sovereignty and human evil is a mystery for the ages, but I'm hoping you'll see that what must have felt entirely out of God's will for Joseph (arriving in Egypt) was actually part of God's plan (Israel enslaved in Egypt for four hundred years).

We simply can't imagine God's reach.

Whether Joseph knew about God's revelation to Abraham or not, what information do we find at the top of Genesis 39:2 that will prove to change everything? Lord was with Joseph

Whenever you see the name LORD in small caps in your Bible, it means *Yahweh*, the personal name of God. It's a name that would remind Israel of the covenant God made with them and of His self-existence, among other realities. The fact that the God of Israel was with Joseph in the far away and pagan land of Egypt is so profound and comforting, there's no way to overstate it. We simply can't imagine God's reach.

What two things about the LORD does Potiphar recognize, according to Genesis 39:3? Lord was with him and made him prosper

PERSONAL TAKE: We're not given much detail, but how do you think Potiphar was able to clearly tell that God was with Joseph?

Joseph worshipped God - had a relationship w/ God Trusted God

According to the passages below, what will cause others to see Jesus in our lives? Write your response next to each reference.

❑ John 13:34-35

love one another

❑ 1 Thessalonians 1:4-7

patience, faith in trouble

Looking closely at Genesis 39:5, what was on Potiphar's household and all that he owned? The Lord's _____, circle the correct answer below:

Revelation   (Blessing)   Kindness   Judgment

> *Certain blessings can only come in the midst of our suffering.*

In our western culture, we tend to think of God's blessing and our suffering as mutually exclusive. We think of blessing as all the good things happening in the middle of all the good times. But in Joseph's story we discover something that challenges our mind-set, even as believers: Certain blessings can only come in the midst of our suffering. In Egypt, Joseph was rising in power and position. He had found favor with his master, and his work was prospering. Still, all these blessings fell upon Joseph in a land far away from his family and in a culture that didn't worship his God. The blessings were abounding in the midst of His suffering.

I remember a time when I was hurting so badly that I refused to receive the blessings the Lord was bringing me in that season. I wanted Him to give me what I wanted and wasn't willing to "settle" for anything different. It wasn't until I chose to accept His path for my healing and His way of blessing that I began to change. I didn't get what I so desperately wanted, but all these years later I wouldn't dare exchange the blessings He's given me for what I once demanded of Him.

PERSONAL RESPONSE: Are you refusing God's blessings in the midst of your trial? Take some time to surrender your pain to the Lord. Tell Him you're willing to receive His blessings even if they look different than what you're hoping for. Thank Him for His presence with you, and ask Him to manifest that presence so that it brings you peace, comfort, and joy.

Next week we'll begin an exciting five days of study in the next chapter of Joseph's life. Take some time to process what you've learned and experienced this week because the story line ahead will be as rich as the one we've just covered. Keep asking the Holy Spirit to teach His Word to you, and thank Him for His presence on the journey.

SESSION 2 VIEWER GUIDE

THE UNLIKELY PATH OF BLESSING

GROUP DISCUSSION

What portion of the video teaching really resonated with you? Why?

Discuss the many ways favoritism damaged Jacob's family. How is it damaging to our relationships?

God created a path of blessing out of Joseph's difficult circumstances. How have you seen Him do this in your life?

It seemed as though God had lost control of Joseph's story. How does God's presence with Joseph encourage you that He is with us even in our hardest seasons?

Why do we often evaluate God's presence and work in our lives based on our circumstances? What would be a more biblical approach?

How has God evidenced His presence in your life in your most difficult moments?

God's blessing on Joseph spilled over onto Potiphar's house. How does this inspire you to bless those who don't yet know Jesus with the blessings He's given you?

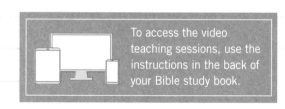

To access the video teaching sessions, use the instructions in the back of your Bible study book.

Classic Fiesta Dip (serves 10–12)

INGREDIENTS

1 teaspoon olive oil

½ onion, chopped

1 clove garlic, minced

16 ounces ground beef

Salt and black pepper, to taste

1 (16-ounce) package cream cheese,
  softened

1 (4.5-ounce) can chopped green chilies

1 (8-ounce) package mushrooms, diced

1 (15-ounce) can pinto beans, drained and rinsed

1 (14-ounce) jar salsa

2 cups shredded mozzarella cheese

1 cup shredded cheddar cheese

Everyone needs a fiesta dip recipe handy should a gathering suddenly arise. You can layer this dip or serve the ingredients side by side for a more visually pleasing presentation. This recipe, along with a companion recipe for homemade beans, is included in Kelly's cookbook, *A Place at the Table*. You can't go wrong.

DIRECTIONS

Preheat your oven to 350 degrees.

In a skillet over medium-high heat, warm the olive oil. Add the onion and garlic, sautéeing for about 3 minutes.

Add the beef and cook, using a wooden spoon to break apart the meat. Add salt and pepper to taste, and cook until brown. Set aside.

In a 13x9-inch baking dish, layer the ingredients. Start with cream cheese, spreading in an even layer on the bottom of the dish. Then layer the ground beef mixture, green chilies, mushrooms, pinto beans, and salsa. Top with the mozzarella and cheddar cheeses.

Bake at 350 degrees for about 30 minutes or until the cheese is bubbly. Serve warm with tortilla chips.

FAITHFUL IN BROKENNESS

The street I live on is peppered with old-timers and relative newcomers like myself. Its rich diversity runs end to end. We're a front porch dwelling collection of friends and acquaintances who often stop to chat, especially during the spring and summer months when everyone's outdoors tending grills, pulling weeds, or pushing strollers up and down the hill. Miss Johnson was the queen of conversation, the unofficial mayor of our neighborhood, and the retired head of the beautifying committee. Rarely could you pass her house without receiving some sort of a resounding greeting or inquiry from her. "Well now, Kelly," she'd say to me, "How are them tomatoes doing this year?" Translation: *Bring me some tomatoes right now, young lady.* When Miss Johnson suddenly had a stroke, it was a neighborhood affair. I encountered the trove of long-standing relationships on our street— relationships she'd helped us build. Miss Johnson is now housebound and unable to see, walk, or feed herself. We all miss her personality so. But none misses it as much as her best friend, Miss Meyers.

The other day I visited with Miss Meyers, who lives just a few doors down from me. She told me that she'd just been by to visit Miss Johnson. "Oh darling, it's so hard to go in there," she lamented. "Hard to see my best friend that way. It takes every single thing I got just to stay in there thirty minutes, having to watch her suffer." She paused for a moment. "But you know what Jesus says, now don't-cha? 'When I was sick, you visited Me. Whatever you do unto the least of these, you do unto *Me.*'" Miss Meyers's eighty-something-year-old finger pointed my direction as she spoke. Somehow I didn't feel scolded in the least. I felt reminded, reminded of the important message God tells us from the beginning of Scripture to the end: love one another with everything you've got because this is how Jesus loves you.

Sometimes we mistakenly think the God of the Old Testament suddenly got nice when the Jesus of the New Testament showed up. But God has *always* cared about the poor, outcast, outsider, and sick. He's *always* commanded His people to sacrificially love others. I'm anxious for you to follow Joseph's story this week because even Joseph's own suffering won't give him a pass from loving the people around him. In fact, we'll find him serving others in the midst of his pain, and this ministry will prove to be some of his most significant.

I'm glad I strolled by Miss Meyers's this week, glad she wasn't afraid to do a little preaching to me about Jesus' command to love others, in particular our sweet friend Miss Johnson. And I'm glad that this week Joseph won't let us forget God has been in the business of love all along.

DAY 1
TEMPTATION
GENESIS 39:6-18

It seems we are never more susceptible to a major act of sin than when we're suffering. Welcome to Session 3 of our study on the life of Joseph. I wasn't sure how to ease you into our subject matter for today, so I'm going with the ever present option of jumping straight in—sometimes pleasantries are overrated. Today we'll be looking at the particularly human experience of temptation. Several places in Scripture tell us how to deal with temptation, I'm grateful Joseph shows us how.

TAKE YOUR TIME WITH THE TEXT TODAY. READ GENESIS 39:1-18. (YOU READ VERSES 1-6 AT THE CLOSE OF LAST WEEK, BUT REFRESH YOUR MEMORY BY BEGINNING WITH VERSE 1 TODAY.)

Verse 6 gives us some important details. What does this verse tell us about Joseph's authority and power in Potiphar's house?

Joseph is head of all - Potiphar has trusted him

What does this verse tell us about Joseph's appearance? good looking

PERSONAL TAKE: How can the combination of these two characteristics sometimes be problematic, especially if someone is not yielded to the Lord?

> *How could I do this immense evil, and how could I sin against God?*
>
> Genesis 39:9b

I found one scholar's description humorous: "Amid Joseph's many blessings, he suffers from one endowment too many, stunning beauty."[1] I keep thinking to myself, *if only I could suffer more from stunning beauty.* The literal translation used to describe Joseph's handsome appearance is "fair with regard to form."[2] It's similar to how his mother, Rachel, is described in Genesis 29:17 as well as Queen Esther in Esther 2:7.[3]

What do we find out in verse 10 about how long Potiphar's wife seduced Joseph?

every day

The length of temptation is often part of what makes temptation so tempting. It's hard to resist something desirable over and over again. It's hard to say no for a long season. We'll talk about this more at the end of today's study.

READ GENESIS 2:15-17.

We're often tempted by the one thing we're not supposed to have. In Adam and Eve's case, God withheld nothing from them except the tree of the knowledge of good and evil. In Joseph's case, Potiphar withheld nothing from Joseph except Potiphar's wife.

PERSONAL TAKE: Eve saw God as selfishly withholding from her. Why do you think Joseph didn't view Potiphar's wife as something God was withholding from him? *Joseph knew God had blessed him since being in Egypt*

Returning to today's text, list all the reasons Joseph gave for not sleeping with Potiphar's wife (vv. 8-9). How do you think each of them strengthened him to stand firm?

not to sin against God
Potiphar's trust

PERSONAL TAKE: It's easy to gloss over the immense pressure and length of this temptation when quickly reading through these verses. I want to keep us from doing that. Pause for a moment, and list every reason you can think of why Joseph would have been particularly vulnerable to sleeping with Potiphar's wife. (Consider how he could have wrongly "justified" this action.)

Have you ever given into temptation because you thought you deserved the person or pleasure it was offering? Have you succumbed because God "hasn't shown up" for you in a while? Has your situation become so lonely and your rejection so painful that you think, *surely my actions are justified*? I've been there, and I understand that struggle from a deeply empathetic place in my heart. That's why I'm thankful God preserved this part of Joseph's story for us. Joseph's reasons for resisting temptation during a lonely and painful time can help protect us from temptation's harm.

In what ways did Joseph believe that sleeping with Potiphar's wife would affect the following individuals (vv. 8-9)? (Some connections will be clearer than others so just do your best.)
❑ *Potiphar:*

❑ *Potiphar's Wife:*

❑ *Himself:*

❑ *God:*

If Joseph had fallen to this temptation, he would have betrayed his master, abused his power with Potiphar's wife, brought guilt upon himself, and above all, sinned against God. Joseph treasured His relationship with the Lord and didn't want to sin against Him. He valued Potiphar and the role he'd been given in Potiphar's house. Joseph's integrity mattered. It's not explicitly stated in the text here, but I also believe Joseph respected Potiphar's wife enough not to have a sexual relationship with her. When faced with temptation, considering the consequences and impact sin will have on our relationship with God, with others, and ourselves will help keep us from giving in.

READ PSALM 51:1-12.

Who did David say he'd sinned against after his affair with Bathsheba? Why do you think he singled God out? God

> *When faced with temptation, considering the consequences and impact sin will have on our relationship with God, with others, and ourselves will help keep us from giving in.*

PERSONAL RESPONSE: Based on this psalm, name some of the consequences David had to deal with that Joseph spared himself from.

loss of respect, lost a child, lost a wife

LOOK BACK AT GENESIS 39:10-12.

How did Joseph escape this final temptation from Potiphar's wife?

fled from her

READ 1 CORINTHIANS 10:13.

How does this verse relate to Joseph's actions?

*He was able to escape
not tempted beyond what he could resist*

What four truths does Paul reveal to us in 1 Corinthians 10:13?

1. The temptations that come upon us are Common to Mean

2. God is faithful.

3. God will not allow us to be tempted beyond what We are able to withstand

4. With temptation, God will also provide a way out.

Have you ever thought that the wayward desires you're experiencing are different from all others'? It's just like the enemy to tell you that you're the only one who deals with a particular temptation. This blatant lie will cause you to feel powerless against temptation, as if giving in is your only option. On the other hand, we're empowered when we humble ourselves enough to recognize that every temptation we deal with is something others have experienced and are experiencing. Your temptation is not unique.

Also, God always provides a way out. I never tire of the fact that God's way of escape for Joseph was something as simple and nondescript as the door. The word *door* isn't mentioned specifically, but the author tells us that Joseph ran outside—which I assume was through a door. My point is: I've often hoped God would provide me with a way of escape by means of an angel, a miraculous and instantaneous dose of willpower, or some other supernatural happening. But God gave Joseph two legs to run with and a door of escape to run through. That was all he needed.

PERSONAL REFLECTION: How have you played games with temptation instead of simply fleeing it? If you're in a tempting situation now, detail your plan of escape. According to Paul, the Lord has already provided you with one.

Dearest friends, if I could leave you with anything today, it's this: **don't let your suffering lead to sinning.** As we said at the start of this day's study, we're especially vulnerable to sin when we're in the middle of pain. So let's be on our guard, especially when we're hurting. And remember, God is never the source or author of our temptation (Jas. 1:13). I want to close today's study with three truths I've learned from this part of Joseph's life and through my own life experiences.

1. God's boundaries are good boundaries.

Joseph believed that God's boundaries were good, and this belief kept him from sinning. I wonder if you, like me, have ever questioned whether or not God really has your best in mind. When we believe that His commands are good, we'll be less likely to cross the lines He's set for our safety and flourishing.

2. Our sin is first and foremost against God.

Many times I've fled from temptation simply because I knew the consequences would be overwhelming. As I've grown in my relationship with Jesus, my reasons for avoiding temptation now have more to do with how costly sin would be to my intimacy with Him. If your main reason for not sinning has to do with the consequences, it's not a bad reason but it's an incomplete one. While it's always good to flee temptation, only your love for Christ will keep you on a lifelong path of devotion and obedience to Him.

3. All temptation eventually comes to an end.

Joseph's temptation went on day after day, a detail that shows duration of time as well as intensity. Temptation is often oppressive and relentless, as it was in Joseph's case. But eventually his temptation came to an end and so will yours.

PERSONAL RESPONSE: What is God speaking to you about today? If there's a temptation you need to flee from, take a page out of Joseph's book and run for your life in the other direction, even if it means leaving something dear behind. Nothing you lose while fleeing will compare to what you might lose if you give in to sin or what you will gain in obedience. Let a trusted friend know about your struggle or ask some people who love you to keep you accountable.

Perhaps one of our greatest acts of worship is obeying God in the midst of our pain.

We've begun Session 3 on an intense note, but I believe we may have avoided some devastating consequences of sin today. By committing to following God's way of escape when temptation feels perfectly overwhelming, we're actively putting our faith in Him instead of what feels natural to us. As we'll see throughout our study, the choices Joseph made during this season of temptation would pay off immeasurably for the rest of his life. Perhaps one of our greatest acts of worship is obeying God in the midst of our pain.

DAY 2
GOD'S KINDNESS
GENESIS 39:19-23; 40:1-4

Today we're entering a new stretch in Joseph's story. After faithfully withstanding the temptations of Potiphar's wife, Joseph's world is about to change yet again. A special passage awaits you, so I'll let you get straight to the text.

BEGIN YOUR READING IN GENESIS 39:13-20 EVEN THOUGH YOU READ SOME OF THIS YESTERDAY.

PERSONAL REFLECTION: Picture yourself in Joseph's situation. You remained faithful and obedient to God during a season of temptation. Yet, now you find yourself falsely accused and thrown in prison as a result. Describe how you would feel about your relationship with God and perhaps your faith as a whole?

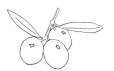

But the LORD was with Joseph and extended kindness to him. He granted him favor with the prison warden.

Genesis 39:21

Just when you thought Joseph's circumstances couldn't bring him any lower, he was thrown in prison. Scholars have pointed out an interesting trajectory of Joseph's life up to this point: He went down into the pit where his brothers threw him; He went down to Egypt after being sold; He went down into prison.[4] It seems that Joseph's compass is continually pointed south, and I know that some of you feel as though your life might be following that same heading.

I've felt that way, too. When something goes wrong, I have to fend off thoughts like, *How come this always happens to me?* Or, *This is so my life!* Or, as we like to say in our family, *This is a total Minter.* My prayer for us is to break out of the woe-is-me cycle as we look not only at Joseph's faithfulness in suffering, but God's kindness to Joseph in the midst of it. We're going to take a sword to self-wallowing today and find joy where we are because God is with us.

CONTINUE READING, IN GENESIS 39:21-23.

According to verse 21, who went to prison with Joseph?

Being The Lord

Detail some of the ways that God showed kindness to Joseph (vv. 21-23).

he found favor w/ the keeper of the prison

PERSONAL REFLECTION: Do you have a hard time enjoying God's presence and accepting His kindness in the midst of your suffering? Explain why or why not.

Over the years, I've realized there's a difference between God's kindness and His deliverance. In our trying circumstances, all we want is for God to deliver us. But sometimes He chooses to keep us where we are so we can learn the blessing of His presence and His specific kindness to us in our trials. When that day of deliverance finally does come, we'll be ready for what's on the other side.

What phrase is mentioned twice in Genesis 39:21-23, and why do you think the author chose to emphasize it? *The Lord was with him*

PERSONAL RESPONSE: What evidences of God's presence and kindness can you identify in your current trial(s)? Pause and thank Him for these—a spirit of gratitude will combat the natural tendency to turn inward and become self-focused.

CONTINUE READING, IN GENESIS 40:1-4.

If we look at this part of the story through a human lens, we will only see an abandoned Joseph whose obedience and faithfulness had gotten him nowhere but in a prison. But if we see the story line through "the wider scheme of God's purposes,"[5] it's "at the nadir [the lowest point] of his life"[6] that Joseph comes "into contact with persons from the apex of Egyptian society."[7] In simpler terms, sometimes the Lord has to take us lower to orchestrate His bringing us to future, breathtaking heights. Will you trust Him where He has you?

Sometimes the Lord has to take us lower to orchestrate His bringing us to future, breathtaking heights.

Oh, and I should mention that trusting God doesn't mean laying back, doing nothing, eating chips, and binge-watching television while you wait for God to get you outta here! God never tables His call on your life. There's always work to be done.

What specific role did Joseph have while in prison (v. 4)?

take care of prisoners

To be the chief cupbearer or baker in Pharaoh's court was to hold a prominent position of influence. (Later in Scripture we find that Nehemiah was cupbearer to King Artaxerxes.) The cupbearer opened and tasted the wine, ensuring its quality before serving it to Pharaoh.[8] The baker was in charge of a vast variety of baked goods in the royal palace.[9] The captain of the guards, possibly Potiphar (Gen. 39:1), assigned Joseph to these men (your Bible translation may say *appointed* or *put in charge of*). As a young Hebrew slave, Joseph was a servant to high-ranking Egyptian officials.

Have you ever been unhappy with the people God has assigned you to? Have you ever thought, *I could do a bang-up job for the Lord if He had just given me different family members, more efficient coworkers, a better church*? Joseph's faithfulness in the assignments God gave him challenges me because he didn't put conditions on God. He humbly attended two people from a foreign country who served other gods and would have naturally despised his Hebrew heritage.

PERSONAL REFLECTION: Is there someone God has called you to love and serve whom you simply don't want to? Write about the relationship below.

The psalmist gives us additional information about what God was accomplishing in Joseph's life during his days in the prison.

> He called down famine against the land and destroyed the entire food supply. He had sent a man ahead of them— Joseph, who was sold as a slave. They hurt his feet with shackles; his neck was put in an iron collar. Until the time his prediction came true, the word of the LORD tested him.

PSALM 105:16-19

The word *tested* here means, *to refine, purify, remove the impurities.* It also means, "to purge gold or silver by fire, and to separate from dross."[10]

PERSONAL TAKE: What insight does the psalmist give us about this particular time in Joseph's life? What was God accomplishing in Joseph?

God doesn't test us so He can find out what's in our hearts—He already knows that. And He doesn't test us to see whether we're going to pass or fail as if He were a calculus professor. He tests us to grow us, strengthen us, and refine us. The imagery of gold being purified by fire references a certain process of purification. The testing doesn't depend on what's passing through the fire, but the sureness of the fire to remove the impurities.

The famous English preacher C. H. Spurgeon said the following about Psalm 105: "There is a trying word and a delivering word, and we must bear the one till the other comes to us."[11] As we considered yesterday, suffering naturally causes us to long for that delivering word and praise God when it comes! But sometimes we need to receive the purifying and sanctifying words of God until that deliverance arrives.

What had Joseph's dreams predicted about his future? (Look back at Genesis 37:5-10 to refresh your memory.) others will bow down to him!

God was not the source of the lies and deceptions from Potiphar's wife. He did not create Potiphar's fury, the fury that led Potiphar to throw Joseph in prison unjustly. However, I do believe that God used this evil to make Joseph ready for the grand tasks ahead.

PERSONAL REFLECTION: How do you see Joseph's time in the prison as a refiner's fire preparing him for what was coming, bringing him forth as gold? understanding others, trusting God

God often uses suffering to make us fit for the dreams He has for us. The question is, Are you willing to comply with the Lord during these seasons of testing? Genesis 39:21-23 reveals that God was with Joseph, had given him tremendous favor, and made his work successful. The tiny problem with all this favor and blessing was that Joseph experienced it inside a prison. Here we discover that blessing and suffering are not mutually exclusive. In fact, sometimes our greatest blessings will be found in our darkest dungeons (Isa. 45:3).

> *God often uses suffering to make us fit for the dreams He has for us.*

PERSONAL RESPONSE: If you're willing to serve God faithfully right where you are, write out a prayer below dedicating yourself and your circumstances to Him. Claim His presence with you and favor upon you.

Dear Lord Help me to remember in times of suffering and uncertainty to remember your faithfulness, love and desire to make me an instrument of your peace, kindness, love

DAY 3
FORGOTTEN BUT NOT FORSAKEN
GENESIS 40:5-23

Sometimes I'm exceptionally keen to God's work in my life and surroundings. In those times almost every encounter seems divinely inspired, Scripture is leaping off the page, and every worship song at church is my favorite. Then there are all the other times—when God is working because He says He is, but I don't necessarily see it or sense it.

The other day I was praying about a ministry endeavor that's been challenging for me the past couple of years. And when I say challenging, it's been like trying to inch a boulder up a hill, afraid that at any moment it's gonna roll back on top of me. In some ways I feel like I'm the only one pushing, while God is carrying everyone else's dreams on eagles' wings to the peaks of mountains. (This may be the drama talking.) Intellectually I know this isn't true, but sometimes it feels true. If you can relate, you'll especially appreciate today's reading.

READ GENESIS 40:5-19.

PERSONAL TAKE: Joseph was young, a slave, and a Hebrew—three reasons the cupbearer and baker wouldn't have respected him or thought of him as someone who could interpret their dreams. Interpreting dreams was something only the highest and brightest of Egypt would dare tackle. Given what you've learned about Joseph so far, what do you think the cupbearer saw in Joseph that caused the cupbearer to share his dream with Joseph?

Trust i caring

We know from other verses that Joseph spent at least two years in the prison and that God was at work every single day Joseph was there. What we don't think as much about are the ways God was simultaneously working on the outside where the rest of the world was going about their lives—the part Joseph couldn't see.

Who did the cupbearer and baker work for before being thrown in prison? (See Gen. 40:2 to refresh your memory.) How might this detail be a strategic part of God's plan for Joseph? (You don't need to know the rest of the story to answer this question.) Pharoah

Look back at verse 5 and fill in the blank.
Each dream had its own interpretation.

According to verse 8, why were the cupbearer and baker distressed? no interpreter for their dream

In verse 6, the word *distraught* (or dejected, troubled) that's used to describe the state of the two officials is a strong Hebrew word. It can mean *a raging storm, anger, or a state of discouragement that is so strong one's appearance is affected.*[12] This word describes the internal and external condition of so many people we know, doesn't it? The cupbearer and baker weren't able to make sense of their dreams, and it was causing them tremendous distress. How often are we distraught because we can't make sense of something?

When Joseph noticed the two officials were distraught, how did he respond (v. 7)? (Circle the best answer below.)

Reprimanded them   *Encouraged them*
Asked them a question   *Fed them*

Taking notice of people, asking them how they're doing, and being a good listener are some of the most powerful ministry acts we can offer. In our busy society we either don't make time to ask others how they're doing, or we simply avoid asking them because we're afraid they might actually tell us! And then what would be required of us? *Better not to ask*, we think.

PERSONAL RESPONSE: Is someone you know distraught right now? When can you take a quiet moment to ask how he or she is really doing? Are you willing to listen to, encourage, and serve that person in the ways the Holy Spirit prompts you? Describe below.

Taking notice of people, asking them how they're doing, and being a good listener are some of the most powerful ministry acts we can offer.

I have dreams all the time that I have no explanation for. By the time I get to my French press in the mornings, I've usually forgotten about them. In Joseph's time, however, dreams were considered one of the primary ways a person received divine revelation. In Pharaoh's court, professional magicians and counselors were tapped to reveal the meaning of these dreams. The chief cupbearer and baker were not distraught because they'd had dreams but because they were cut off from the men they believed could interpret their dreams. Joseph, the Hebrew slave boy, was their only hope. (If you're going through this Bible study as a younger woman, take courage from Joseph's example and also from Paul's words to his young son in the faith, Timothy, in 1 Tim. 4:12).

PERSONAL TAKE: If God is the only One who can interpret dreams, why do you think Joseph told the men to share their dreams with him instead of with God (v. 8)? *They were not believers in god*

While it seems natural for Joseph to credit God as the interpreter of dreams, the Egyptians didn't worship the one true God. They depended on their own wise men and scientists for such divine interpretations. Here Joseph was introducing the God of his Hebrew fathers to pagan Egyptians. Anyone see an early glimpse of the gospel here?

Describe the meanings of each person's dream respectively, according to Joseph:

❏ *Chief Cupbearer* *Restored*

❏ *Chief Baker* *killed*

Verses 14-15 offer us a first glimpse into Joseph's heart and thoughts. Up until this point, we haven't received any insight into Joseph's feelings about the injustice he's experienced. Stating his innocence Joseph says, "I have done nothing that they should put me in the dungeon" (Gen. 40:15b). The word used for *dungeon* is the same word used in 37:20 to describe the cistern Joseph's brothers threw him into. In other words, Joseph is basically saying, *I've gone from dungeon to dungeon!*[13]

PERSONAL REFLECTION: How do these verses help you better understand what Joseph was going through internally?

What event (that took place outside the prison) caused Pharaoh to elevate the cupbearer? his birthday

This seemingly insignificant detail shows that God can use even the most commonplace happenings such as anniversaries, birthdays, promotions, holidays, and so on to orchestrate His divine plan. The cupbearer and baker's dreams happened three days before Pharaoh threw a big birthday bash for himself. The planning of the party must have made him think about the two officials he'd thrown in prison, the ones whose jobs revolved around feasting. We don't know why Pharaoh restored the one and not the other, but it's important for us to know that while God was interpreting dreams for Joseph in prison, He was also working outside the prison. We can't always see what God is doing, but, like Joseph, we can choose to be faithful where we are and trust Him.

> *Look up the following references and write down what you discover about God's care for the oppressed and distressed:*
> ❏ *Psalm 18:16-19*
>
> ❏ *Psalm 27:7-14*
>
> ❏ *Psalm 31:9-24*
>
> ❏ *Psalm 61:1-4*
>
> ❏ *Psalm 107:10-16 (This particular psalm speaks of suffering as a result of rebellion, but even here, note God's response.)*

I don't know what you're going through right now. You may be the victim of gross injustice with no human able to help you. You may have been falsely accused. You may have been plagued with abuse from an early age. You may feel forgotten by God, seemingly going from dungeon to dungeon. My hope is that you'll find comfort in the words of the psalmists and in the desperate pleas of Joseph. This life is not without evil. We were never promised a road without suffering, in fact Jesus assures us that suffering is part of what comes with the sacred call of being one of His followers. "I have told you these things," Jesus says, "so that in me you may have peace. You will have suffering in this world. Be courageous! I have conquered the world" (John 16:33).

Today, I pray you will embrace the truth that God has not left you alone. He has not forgotten you. He sees you. He knows you, and He's mindful of every injustice that's ever been done to you. He is also powerful, able to turn away your enemies, to deliver and establish you. He is not weak concerning you. He is profoundly strong to save. One day, His delivering word will come for you as it's about to come for Joseph in his story. Until then, lean into God's presence, rest under His favor, and let Him purify you until His trying word becomes His delivering word, and you realize you've emerged as purified gold. Fine gold.

Embrace the truth that God has not left you alone. He has not forgotten you. He sees you. He knows you.

DAY 4
DELIVERANCE
GENESIS 41:1-16

Before you begin reading chapter 41 today, look back at Genesis 40:23. Since today's passage is one of hope and deliverance I don't want you to forget how hopeless the situation seemed to be.

The cupbearer failed Joseph. The narrator describes this single failing in two ways. Write them both below.

Did not remember him
Forgot him

PERSONAL TAKE: How does this double emphasis describe the total failure of human help in this situation? *Weakness, disrespect*

Just for the record, I don't think it was wrong for Joseph to plead with the cupbearer to help him. He had a connection to the cupbearer and leaned on that relationship in hopes that the cupbearer could plead Joseph's case to Pharaoh. This feels like wisdom to me. Just because the cupbearer failed Joseph doesn't mean he was wrong for asking. It does, however, remind me of human frailty and selfishness, and it makes me think of a few of my favorite verses in the Book of Psalms that describe God's all-sufficient power in contrast to the utter limitations of human beings.

> It is better to take refuge in the LORD than to trust in humanity.
> It is better to take refuge in the LORD than to trust in nobles.

PSALM 118:8-9

> Do not trust in nobles, in a son of man, who cannot save.
> When his breath leaves him, he returns to the ground; on that
> day his plans die. Happy is the one whose help is the God of
> Jacob, whose hope is in the LORD his God.

PSALM 146:3-5

> He is not impressed by the strength of a horse; he does not
> value the power of a warrior. The LORD values those who fear
> him, those who put their hope in his faithful love.

PSALM 147:10-11

People will fail us for a multitude of reasons. Sometimes their failures are a result of the evil in their hearts and other times it's simply due to the limitations that are inherent to being human.

PERSONAL REFLECTION: Is there a person you're continually hoping will be your savior? If this is the case, reflect on the previous verses from the Psalms. Confess this idolatry to Christ. Tell Him that He is your help and salvation. Determine to shift your focus from this person to Jesus. Jesus is infinitely more able than "the cupbearer" in your life, and He will never forget you. (If you need to spend time working this out with the Lord, skip the rest of today's study and come back to it later.)

Then Pharaoh sent for Joseph, and they quickly brought him from the dungeon. He shaved, changed his clothes, and went to Pharaoh.

Genesis 41:14

NOW WE'RE READY FOR THE PINNACLE OF CHAPTER 41. READ GENESIS 41:1-16.

For how many years had the cupbearer been out of prison and forgotten Joseph?   2 yrs.

Those days and months must have crawled by for Joseph, but God never left him, nor did God stop working on Joseph's behalf. An ancient midrash (commentary on the Scripture) describes the cupbearer's forgetting Joseph from God's perspective, "You may have forgotten [Joseph], but I have not forgotten him." [14]

Paraphrase Pharaoh's dreams in the columns below:

COWS FROM THE NILE	HEADS OF GRAIN
Fat cows eaten by lean ones	healthy sheaths eaten by unhealthy ones

LOOK BACK AT VERSE 8.

What two groups of people were responsible for hearing and interpreting dreams? magicians, wisemen

Once Pharaoh told these men his dreams, who precisely was able to help him? None

In Egyptian culture, magicians were trained to interpret dreams. They studied the ritual books of magic to help them interpret symbolic images. They practiced divination and, in some instances, were able to replicate the supernatural, like in Exodus 7:11. The wise men were well-educated advisors who additionally offered guidance to Pharaoh as ones who were helped by the gods.[15]

While the cupbearer and baker were distressed that none of the dream experts were around to help them interpret their dreams, Pharaoh had every one of them at his disposal! Still, they were incapable. (This is reminiscent of the pain and depravity that seems to be increasing around us despite the very resourced country we live in.) Only the one true God with whom Joseph had an intimate relationship would be able to provide Pharaoh with an answer.

SLOWLY TAKE IN VERSES 8-14 AGAIN.

Why did the cupbearer suddenly remember Joseph? because of his dream

How did Joseph's prior ministry to the cupbearer suddenly play a significant role in Joseph's deliverance? he was remembered

PERSONAL REFLECTION: How does God's faithfulness encourage you to continue to love and serve others even in the midst of your own difficulties?

This part of Joseph's story reminds me of Hebrews 6:10: "For God is not unjust; he will not forget your work and the love you demonstrated for his name by serving the saints—and by continuing to serve them." Although this verse is within the context of serving other believers, the truth that God never forgets our labor of love remains.

Maybe you've been serving others for a long time with no outward signs of appreciation. God is not unjust; He will not forget your love. Maybe you've been helping others in your own season of hurt. God is not unjust; He will not forget your love. Perhaps you wonder if your sacrifice is making any difference at all. God is not unjust; He will not forget your love.

I NEVER TIRE OF READING GENESIS 41:14.
What outward changes did Joseph make? Shaved, changed clothes

Describe the pace at which Joseph was brought from the prison.
Quickly

The Hebrew word for *quickly* in verse 14 is derived from the root word for *run*.[16] Suffering can be long but deliverance is often quick. Even though God operates outside of time, I have to believe that God, in His great love for Joseph, had been looking forward to this moment when Joseph's suffering in prison would end in an instant. The trying season had dissolved into deliverance, and it was time for Joseph to do what God had been preparing him for all along.

PERSONAL RESPONSE: How do you see God using your current trial to prepare you for what's ahead? You may not be able to make out all the details, but think about the ways He's making you more like Jesus. patient

READ 1 PETER 1:3-9.

Peter, a disciple of Jesus Christ, wrote those words. He suffered a great deal as a result of following Christ. What are some of the reasons Peter says we'll experience trials?

He's preparing us for what He's prepared for us.

According to verse 7, what will be the result of our suffering as followers of Christ? How does this help you rejoice in your trials?

Sometimes a change in perspective is more powerful than the change we hope for in our circumstances. If we see our trials as curses, punishments, or signs of God's displeasure with us, we'll be in a double heap of pain. But if we, like Peter, see our suffering as the crucible by which our faith in Jesus Christ will prove genuine and bring Him glory, well, that is altogether hopeful.

Joseph changed his clothes, signaling a fresh start and a new beginning. Today, let's take off "the clothes" of self-wallowing, self-centeredness, and despair. Let's choose to focus on the truth that God will not waste a moment of our pain or waiting. He's preparing us for what He's prepared for us.

DAY 5
REFRAMING YOUR INADEQUACY

GENESIS 41:17-36

It is God who will give Pharaoh a favorable answer.

Genesis 41:16b

When I was in my late twenties, I attended an event where my friend Angela Thomas-Pharr taught on the concept of waiting for it to be your turn. At that age, I desperately wanted it to be my turn—to sing, write, teach, have success, be financially stable, you name it. What would have helped me during those years was a deeper confidence that God was preparing me during the waiting, an understanding that all those long years were leading somewhere. You may be waiting for it to be your turn, too. (Each of us is in some stage of waiting.) As we continue to study Joseph's life, I hope it's increasingly clear to you that it's in the waiting where God prepares us for what He has for us in the future. So when it's our turn, we'll be ready.

Today it's Joseph's turn.

> READ GENESIS 41:15-36. I'M HAVING YOU READ A COUPLE VERSES FROM YESTERDAY TO REMIND YOU OF THE CONTEXT.

PERSONAL REFLECTION: How had Joseph's preparation during his waiting qualified him to answer Pharaoh's impossible request?

The Egyptian magicians were expected to hear a dream and be able to interpret it. How did Joseph see his qualifications as being very different from theirs (v. 16)? He believed in Gods

Joseph's response in Genesis 41:16a, "I am not able to" (CSB) (or "I cannot do it" [NIV] or "It is not in me" [ESV]) is a single word in Hebrew, *bil'aday.*[17] In one word he summed up the concept we've all felt a thousand times when faced with someone else's impossible situation: *I don't have what it takes.* Don't you wish we had this single word in English? Think of how much less talking we'd have to do. Joseph's response is absolutely remarkable here. He is lightning quick to set Pharaoh's expectations straight: without God, Joseph has nothing for Pharaoh.

PERSONAL REFLECTION: What God-given task do you currently feel inadequate to accomplish? (Think in terms of hanging in there in a difficult marriage, sharing Jesus with a coworker, leading the youth group at your church, raising a child as a single mom, serving as a single woman, and so on.)

LOOK UP 2 CORINTHIANS 3:4-6.

In what ways do you see Paul's words resemble Joseph's response to Pharaoh? It's all God's doing — His sufficiency

I keep returning to Joseph's response and to the 2 Corinthians passage because I feel especially inadequate right now. To name a few examples, I have some friends who practice a religion that's very different from following Christ, and I don't always know how to talk with them about the good news of Jesus. I'm not the clear and decisive leader I wish I were. I have a family member who's suffering from a chronic illness, and several other situations have piled up beyond what I'm able to handle. I keep going back to, *if Christ doesn't do it in me or for me, I've got nothing.*

Joseph was quick to explain to Pharaoh that he wasn't able to interpret dreams, however, he knew the God who could interpret them. I hope someone somewhere is on her sofa with her coffee yelling *AMEN*!

In yesterday's study you detailed Pharaoh's two dreams. Now I want you to explain the symbolism from each dream and its meaning. (See Gen. 41:25-36.)

COWS FROM THE NILE	HEADS OF GRAIN

TRUE/FALSE: *The dreams meant two different things.*

Why did God give Pharaoh the two dreams? (See vv. 25 and 28.)

[handwritten] him in what God is going to do

Pharaoh had all the kingdom's resources in the palm of his hand. He had the magicians and wise men at the snap of his fingers. They had knowledge galore and education for days, but they were missing what the young, Hebrew slave possessed: God-given wisdom.

Detail the wise instruction Joseph gave Pharaoh for handling the coming seven years of abundance and seven years of famine (vv. 33-36).

[handwritten] Store up food

The Hebrew word, *ra`*, the word used to describe the thin and sickly cows, isn't clear in our English translations. But we know the original Hebrew means evil or wicked.[18] Juxtaposed against the good and healthy cows, scholar John H. Sailhamer points out that Pharaoh's dreams tie into one of the central themes of Genesis, the knowledge of good and evil.[19] "Joseph is the embodiment of the ideal that true wisdom, the ability to discern between 'good and evil,' comes only from God."[20]

> *How we need the Holy Spirit who not only helps us discern between good and evil, but also gives us the wisdom to overcome evil with good.*

Sometimes discerning between good and evil is black and white, while other times it's not so simple. How do you know when it's right to stand with the opinions of the day, and when it's not OK? (Try not to give a "Sunday School answer.")

It's easy to get confused in a culture that frequently changes its opinion about what is good and what is evil—for better or worse. We're often faced with situations that are so complicated we don't know when helping is beneficial or when helping is hurting. How we need the Holy Spirit who not only helps us discern between good and evil, but also gives us the wisdom to overcome evil with good.

Read James 1:5-6. How do we as believers get wisdom?

[handwritten] from God

Read Proverbs 9:10. Where does wisdom begin?

[handwritten] Fear of the Lord

Read Proverbs 2:1-6. The author of Proverbs tells us to seek for wisdom as though it's _____silver_____.

PERSONAL RESPONSE: Earlier I asked you what God-given task you feel inadequate to handle. Based on Joseph's story and the additional passages of Scripture we've turned to today, how can you reframe your inadequacy as an opportunity to depend on Jesus? Write a prayer of response below.

Today we saw how aware Joseph was of his limitations. Perhaps it's made you aware of your own. The Lord has recently allowed me to go through a long stretch of running up against my limitations, and it's been a humbling season to say the least. It's also been a time of healing. The more I see how incapable I am in my own strength, the more I'm moved by Jesus' delight in still desiring to use me. His tenderness in wanting me to be dependent upon Him has been restorative for my soul. In Joseph's words, I cannot, but God is able. If this is true for Joseph, how true it is for you and me.

The more I see how incapable I am in my own strength, the more I'm moved by Jesus' delight in still desiring to use me.

SESSION 3 VIEWER GUIDE

FAITHFUL IN BROKENNESS

GROUP DISCUSSION

What portion of the video teaching really resonated with you? Why?

Why are we especially vulnerable to sin in the middle of our pain?

What did Joseph's experience with temptation teach you about how to deal with your own?

God showed kindness to Joseph in the middle of his suffering. If you're in a difficult season, how have you seen God's kindness displayed in the midst of the struggle?

Joseph's suffering helped prepare him for what lay ahead. How has God used your suffering to not only conform you to the image of Christ, but also to prepare you for a specific work?

Why do you think some of our most effective ministry happens in the middle of our suffering?

If people who fail you can't ultimately prevent God's plan for you, how does this free you to let go of bitterness and unforgiveness toward them?

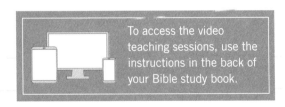

To access the video teaching sessions, use the instructions in the back of your Bible study book.

Mango Salad with Orange Dressing (serves 4–6)

INGREDIENTS

Dressing:

¾ cup vegetable oil

1 tablespoon sugar

1 clove garlic, minced

Salt and black pepper, to taste

4 tablespoons red wine vinegar

1 orange, divided

Salad:

4 cups mixed greens of your choice

2 mangoes, peeled and diced

2 tablespoons walnuts, toasted

Since you can never have enough salad recipes, here's a light and refreshing option, great for when you want to serve something a little special. The mangoes give the salad a nice flare, and the dressing pulls it all together.

DIRECTIONS

For the dressing, whisk together oil, sugar, garlic, salt, pepper, and vinegar. Halve the orange, juicing one half and setting aside the juice. Peel the second half of the orange and cut into segments. Add orange segments and orange juice to the dressing. Chill or store in the refrigerator.

Arrange the greens on a platter, decorate with mango pieces, and top with the dressing and walnuts.

FAITHFUL IN ABUNDANCE

Joseph's hardships were making him fit for the dreams God had for him. To be a ruler in God's economy first meant a stretch of humbling. It also meant building up perseverance's muscles. And, above all, it meant finding God faithful when no one else was. Before Joseph could lead a people or save a nation He had to know—to be convinced of—the all-sufficiency of God's presence with Him.

When I first moved to Nashville, my sincere aim was to be a wildly successful singer/songwriter all for the glory of God. (If you haven't heard, things didn't play out quite by my script). I was pleased to live for the renown of Christ as long as my own fame had solid footing on His stage. Besides the fact that these two goals were directly at odds with one another, I had also somehow missed Jesus' words about the greatest person being the one who serves (Matt. 23:11).

Looking back, I can see my own Nashville wilderness experience—a barren land for many a musician and performer—as God's training ground for what lay ahead. It was a lonely, walls-pressing-in season of life and for reasons far beyond lost record deals. I didn't know it at the time, but God was preparing me to study His Word and impart it to people through writing and speaking, along with a little singing. I couldn't properly do these things without first being humbled. (If it were grammatically acceptable I'd capitalize the "H," because lowercase humbled just doesn't emote enough under the circumstances.) How could I teach the Bible if I hadn't first clung to its pages as if it were a life preserver keeping me afloat? What would I have to say about Jesus if I hadn't yet walked with Him through my own rivers and fires? And how would I know where I was headed in ministry if I didn't grasp the reality that leading through serving is God's upside down way? These discoveries don't usually come to us on a silver platter. Ease doesn't typically sanctify a person.

As we consider Joseph's rise to power, we'll notice His rule would be one of rescue, kindness, and deliverance. He would leverage his influence to sustain lives. If Joseph's heart hadn't been refined in the prison, I don't think he could have reflected the heart of Christ so clearly in the palace. I don't know what future plans God is readying you for, but arriving wherever you're going looking more like Jesus is a destination in and of itself. As we experience this sanctifying transformation, we'll begin to realize that wherever we're headed isn't nearly as thrilling as reflecting Him when we get there.

DAY 1
GOD'S SPIRIT IN YOU
GENESIS 41:37-45

Every year I spend a week in the Amazon jungle at JMI's Annual Jungle Pastor's Conference. More than one hundred native pastors and their wives attend, my personal heroes who are devoted to reaching the *ribeirinhos* (Portuguese word for the people who live along the river) with the gospel of Jesus Christ. We spend several days together learning, worshiping, fellowshiping, and eating. The eating part is a personal favorite—coconut cake made with coconuts that someone just climbed a tree and picked, anyone? No group of people in the world remind me more of Joseph's dependence on the Spirit of God than my dear friends in the Amazon. I'll explain more as we go today.

So Pharaoh said to Joseph, "Since God has made all this known to you, there is no one as discerning and wise as you are."

Genesis 41:39

READ GENESIS 41:37-45. AS YOU READ, ENJOY THE HOPE AND TRANSFORMATION GOD IS BRINGING ABOUT IN JOSEPH'S LIFE.

When Pharaoh promoted Joseph, several things noticeably changed. Each change points us back to a counterpart from Joseph's earlier days. Draw a line between the corresponding descriptions based on verses 40-44.

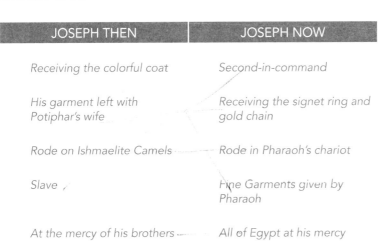

JOSEPH THEN	JOSEPH NOW
Receiving the colorful coat	Second-in-command
His garment left with Potiphar's wife	Receiving the signet ring and gold chain
Rode on Ishmaelite Camels	Rode in Pharaoh's chariot
Slave	Fine Garments given by Pharaoh
At the mercy of his brothers	All of Egypt at his mercy

Joseph likely shaved his facial hair and his head when he was called from prison (Gen. 41:14) in accordance with Egyptian customs at the time. Ironically Hebrews generally only shaved their heads as it related to difficult or painful circumstances. Joseph receiving an extra change of clothing represented his transition from impoverished slave to a person of position. In this Egyptian culture, only the royal house and the wealthy would have had an additional change of clothes, such as this.[1]

Joseph's personal circumstances were dramatically changing to be sure, but we can't miss the much bigger picture of what God was orchestrating for Egypt, the future people of Israel, and ultimately for the world. I may be getting ahead of myself here, but as we drill down into the details of Joseph's life, I never want us to miss what Almighty God is doing from His glorious throne.

PERSONAL REFLECTION: How does this intricate and remarkable turn of events in Joseph's life encourage you to trust God and walk in obedience, even when life is hard and doesn't make sense? Be specific.

He has a plan. He doesn't forget you. He knows what's best

LOOK BACK AT VERSES 37-38.

What distinguished Joseph from everyone else at Pharaoh's disposal (v. 38)?

God's wisdom and advice eloquently power

Based on everything you've read about Joseph so far, what do you think this distinguishing factor might have looked like? In other words, in what ways might the Spirit of God have displayed Himself through Joseph?

patience, wisdom, humility

Pharaoh had the smartest and most educated people at his disposal along with all his kingdom's resources, yet it was the Hebrew slave Joseph who had the one thing no one else in Egypt had—the Spirit of the living God! I only recently recognized this reality while teaching this portion of Joseph's story to the Brazilian pastors' wives in the Amazon.

Like Joseph—before he was pulled from the prison—these women have few possessions to speak of. Many of them are without a permanent home. They're without the world's respect, and some of them are embarrassed to come to the Pastor's Conference because they only have a few changes of clothes. And yet they bless me more than anyone in the world as I see God's Spirit working in them. The day I taught Joseph's story to these remarkable women, I realized: I'm teaching this, but they're living it. (If you've ever experienced something similar as a teacher, you may have fought the urge to light your notes on fire and run for your life.) In that moment, God reminded me that His work in Joseph's life isn't merely an ancient story for us to marvel at. The Holy Spirit is right now looking for men and women through whom He can bring the message of reconciliation to the people in our spheres of influence (2 Cor. 5:18-19). In the Amazon that day, I was standing before a living, breathing group of them.

Sometimes I don't connect the power and presence of the Holy Spirit to the circumstances of my everyday life. Instead of relying on Him, I can easily fall back on my resources. I imagine it can be this way for you, too. So today let's do a refresher study on the Holy Spirit and how He operates in our lives. I've chosen all New Testament passages because I want us to see that since Jesus' coming we now have even greater access to God's Spirit.

The Holy Spirit is right now looking for men and women through whom He can bring the message of reconciliation to the people in our spheres of influence.

READ JOHN 14:15-17,25-26.

In verse 16, Jesus gives the Holy Spirit a special name. What is it?

Helper, the Spirit of Truth

In verse 17, Jesus describes the Holy Spirit as the Spirit of Truth .

NOW TURN TO 1 CORINTHIANS 6:19-20.

In Jewish culture the temple had always been the place of God's dwelling. Now, because of Jesus, the Holy Spirit has taken up residence within you. Don't pass over this reality.

How will this knowledge affect how you treat and use your body today? (You may need to make a specific change based on this truth. If so, describe the change below.)

Respect, don't abuse it

FLIP OVER TO 1 THESSALONIANS 5:19.

What does this verse tell us we can do to the Holy Spirit?

Quench it

READ ROMANS 8:5-6.

What occupies your thoughts? Are they consumed with jealousy, materialism, sexual sin, unforgiveness, comparison thinking? Or are you caught up with the things of the Spirit that promote peace, joy, compassion, kindness, and gentleness? When we purpose to set our minds on the things of the Spirit, we'll naturally walk in accordance with Him.

PERSONAL REFLECTION: Considering the attributes of the Holy Spirit just mentioned, how might you be suppressing His work in your heart?

I quoting things of the Spirit so I can do what I want

READ ROMANS 5:5.

What does the Holy Spirit pour into our hearts? (Circle your answer.)

God's anger   God's peace

God's ~~love~~   God's condemnation

NOW READ 2 CORINTHIANS 3:17.

What always accompanies the Spirit of the Lord?

liberty

AND FINALLY, LET'S LOOK AT LUKE 11:11-13.

What does this passage tell us about God's desire to give us His Holy Spirit?

It is His greatest desire

Great job working your way through these passages. I needed the reminder and I hope you did, too. As we close, let's turn our attention back to Joseph's story.

REREAD GENESIS 41:37-39.

What caused Pharaoh to respond by saying, "Can we find anyone like this, a man who has God's spirit in him" (v. 38)?

Pharaoh recognized Joseph's God-given ability to interpret dreams but that wasn't all he noticed. Pharaoh saw the wisdom of Joseph's plan to save lives. Isn't it interesting that the supernatural, dream-giving, dream-interpreting, all-wise Spirit of God ministered through Joseph in a most practical manner: feeding people who would soon be hungry? As Christ-followers, the wisdom given us by the Holy Spirit should have a practical effect on those around us. Whether we're spending time with the lonely, encouraging someone who's in a difficult situation similar to one we've experienced, opening up our homes, visiting the sick, giving to the poor, or sacrificing for a loved one, the Holy Spirit in our lives should be tangibly evident to the people around us.

Write out a one-sentence summary of Joseph's proposal to Pharaoh for the saving of lives (Gen. 41:33-36). This is from last week's reading.

> *Store up food for reserve during a time of famine*

I don't know where you work, whom you live next to, the people in your family, or the gifts you've been given. But I do know that you've been placed wherever you are to be a blessing to others and to bring honor to Jesus. I'm challenged and inspired by the fact that Joseph didn't only talk about a God who interprets dreams, but he also showed the people around him a God who cares for them and had a plan to save their lives.

You've been placed wherever you are to be a blessing to others and to bring honor to Jesus.

God was working out good through Joseph, good that would overcome the evil of the famine (remember from Day 5, p. 62, of last week the sickly cows that represented the famine derived from the word *evil*).

PERSONAL RESPONSE: What evil do you want to see overcome with good? How does today's study on the Holy Spirit in you encourage you to pray and work toward that end? Describe below.

> *State of the world - Israel & Palestine*

While standing in front of those courageous pastors' wives that day in the Amazon, I realized that what the world desperately needs from us isn't a snappier marketing plan, a bigger budget, better furniture, a cooler wardrobe, or more social media followers (Lord, have mercy on us). The jungle pastors have none of those things. Joseph had none of them. No, the world is desperately seeking men and women with the living God inside them! This is exactly what we as Christ followers have to offer a world that's desperate for the Bread of life in a land of famine. Let's commit to talking and praying about what the Lord is asking us to do. Because you—yes, you—have the Spirit of the living God in you.

DAY 2
THE GOOD YEARS
GENESIS 41:46-52

When Pharaoh pulled a young Hebrew slave from the prison, he did so because Joseph possessed the one thing that no one else in Pharaoh's court had—the Spirit of the living God. The Spirit of God working through Joseph was never supposed to be a phenomenon unique to Joseph in that one brief slice of history. If Joseph was able to bring divine revelation, profound discernment, and godly wisdom to the people of Egypt, how much more should we be able to bring the gospel of Jesus to those around us through the power of the Spirit?

PERSONAL REFLECTION: Before we get into today's reading, what specifically stood out to you in yesterday's personal study about the Holy Spirit's role in your life? *To guide and protect*

READ GENESIS 41:46-52.

How old was Joseph when he entered Pharaoh's service?

30 yo

According to Genesis 37:2, how old was Joseph around the time of his prophetic dreams?

17

Based on this information, approximately how long had Joseph been in Egypt?

13 y.s.

> *We won't serve God in the good times (the palace) if we're not willing to serve Him in the hard times (the prison).*

What must it have been like for Joseph as he rode freely across Egypt's vast and open landscape after having been confined at least two years in a prison? Joseph's faithfulness in both places reminds me that we won't serve God in the good times (the palace) if we're not willing to serve Him in the hard times (the prison). It's just the truth. Joseph was faithful to God in his times of waiting and trial, and now he could be entrusted to lead a nation during abundant prosperity.

PERSONAL REFLECTION: Whether in a trying season or place of abundance, what does being faithful to God look like for you right now? Be specific. *Praying, keeping my focus on Him, being open to His leading, and doing it.*

We often think about how difficult it is to manage our work and personal lives during adversity. It's easy to forget that this can also be challenging in times of surplus and prosperity, too. We can't forget that with seasons of peace, prosperity, and abundance come a wonderful responsibility to steward those blessings.

Look back at Genesis 41:34-35. How are the seven years described in verse 34? *plentiful*

What was required of Joseph during those good years? *to prepare, to gather reserves*

PERSONAL REFLECTION: If you're in a season of peace and prosperity, how are you stewarding these good years for Christ's service? *Saving. Need to reserve also*

So Joseph stored up grain in such abundance—like the sand of the sea—that he stopped measuring it because it was beyond measure.

Genesis 41:49

TO GIVE US A BETTER PICTURE OF JUST HOW ABUNDANT THESE SEVEN GOOD YEARS WERE, LOOK BACK AT GENESIS 41:49.

Why did Joseph stop measuring the grain he'd harvested? *it was beyond measure – plentiful*

I love this imagery. The harvest was so vast, the grain heaped so high, that Joseph gave up even trying to measure it. I can't help but think of Paul's words in Ephesians 3:20-21, "Now to him who is able to do *immeasurably* more than all we ask or imagine, according to his power that is at work within us, to him be glory in the church and in Christ Jesus throughout all generations, for ever and ever! Amen" (NIV, *emphasis mine*).

PERSONAL TAKE: When God pours out His blessing, why do you think He often surpasses our human ability to measure it?

To show His abundant love and goodness and power/ability

An immeasurable amount of grain wasn't the only way God blessed Egypt and prospered Joseph. Let's turn our attention to the dramatic happening in today's Scripture reading, the two sons born to Joseph and his wife, Asenath.

Write the meaning of the names Joseph gave his sons below (vv. 51-52).
Manasseh: God has made me forgetting all and my father's family

Ephraim: — God made Joseph fruitful even away from His family

PERSONAL TAKE: We'll examine Manasseh's name first. What do you think Joseph meant when he said that God had made him forget his previous hardship and his family? (Keep in mind: if Joseph's dreams were to be fulfilled, his father and brothers would bow before him.)

Of course, we know that Joseph hadn't literally forgotten his family or his father. He also hadn't forgotten being thrown in a pit by his brothers, sold, enslaved in Egypt, or left in a prison. The birth of Manasseh didn't suddenly give him amnesia, although I've heard having children can do these things to you. I do wonder, however, if the fulfillment of the dream had been such a long time coming that Joseph questioned whether he'd heard God right. Did Joseph figure having Manasseh was God's new plan that somehow replaced the old dream that included his fathers and brothers? We don't know exactly what Joseph was thinking, but it's worth pondering, especially in light of how our own faith and belief can waiver in long times of waiting. (See Ps. 27:13-14; Isa. 64:4.)

Now let's consider Ephraim. What seems incongruous about the meaning of his name? Put another way, what two ideas don't seem to go together?

Fruitful but not with family

I don't know if you're like me, but I'm always hoping God will make me fruitful in the land of my prosperity, in the land of my happiness, in the land of being married and having children, in the land of a trattoria on every corner. But do you see what's taking place here? God is blessing and prospering Joseph precisely in the place that had once caused him great pain! (And perhaps still did.) I hope you will receive this as encouragement. God will not waste your pain. In fact, God specializes in sowing seeds into the soil of our hardship, seeds that bring forth prolific life and bear fruit in season.

> LOOK UP PSALM 126. IT'S A BRIEF PSALM SO READ ALL SIX VERSES ABOUT THE ISRAELITES BEING BROUGHT BACK TO JERUSALEM FROM CAPTIVITY.

PERSONAL REFLECTION: How does Psalm 126:5-6 along with the birth of Joseph's two sons reveal that God is a good steward of your hardships?

He doesn't forget your hardship and does bring you joy and reward

God will not waste your pain. In fact, God specializes in sowing seeds into the soil of our hardship, seeds that bring forth prolific life and bear fruit in season.

PERSONAL TAKE: Manasseh and Ephraim are both Hebrew names. Why might Joseph have given his sons Hebrew names instead of Egyptian ones? (Does this tell you anything about what Joseph still believed God could do with his story?) *He honored God and his family*

We'll come back to the significance of Manasseh and Ephraim later in our study. Both would play important roles as part of the twelve tribes of Israel and God's redemptive plan throughout the world. The blessing Joseph's sons would be to him and the ways God would multiply them would, much like the grain in Egypt, be perfectly immeasurable. In the meantime, remember that God is able to prosper you in the place of your pain, cultivating life in ways you may never have imagined.

DAY 3
THE POWER OF GOOD
GENESIS 41:53-57

We are figuratively making a cross-cultural journey every time we open our Bibles. When we read Scripture, we often find ourselves in different lands with unfamiliar customs and languages, worlds far away from our own. Today we find Joseph in another situation that's foreign to most of us—famine. The closest I've ever been to a famine is walking to the grocery store in a snowstorm only to find the milk shelves bare and a sign made out of cardboard in the produce section that said, "Yes, we have no bananas."[2] (A very clever reference to the 1923 hit song, for those of you who are one hundred years old.)

One of the benefits of traveling to other parts of the world is meeting people who have lived through Joseph-esque hardships and are still finding God faithful. I once sat with Manoel and Michele, jungle pastors in the Amazon, who told me about the annual floods that wipe out their crops and cause fish to be scarce. They and their children have gone without food many times, leaning solely on God to provide for them. Their testimonies of His provision are nothing short of miraculous. You'll hear their story in this week's video teaching. As we begin today's reading, let's do our best to imagine the desperation these seven years of famine brought about in Joseph's day and also to remember that countless people around the world are currently facing a similar reality today.

READ GENESIS 41:53-57.

TRUE/FALSE: *The famine was in Egypt as well as the surrounding lands.*

When the inhabitants of Egypt cried out to Pharaoh for help, he sent them to Joseph with what specific instruction?

> Do whatever Joseph says to do

PERSONAL TAKE: Why do you think Pharaoh was so drawn to Joseph? Why was he so trusting of Joseph's plan to save Egypt? (Don't even think I'm going to let you get away with just writing, the Holy Spirit. Flesh this out.)

> His assurance, his wisdom, his devotion to god

Today's passage is important as it pertains to God's covenant with Abraham.

TURN TO GALATIANS 3:8-9 TO REVISIT THE NATURE OF THE COVENANT.

Who specifically will be blessed through Abraham? (Circle below.)

Israel   Europe   America   (All Nations)

How do you see this principle already playing out in Joseph's story?

He is serving all lands

Pharaoh's trust in Joseph both fascinates and challenges me. How often do we see people of no faith or people of a distinctly non-Christian faith lean on us, as Christ-followers, for wisdom or trust us for help? It seems the louder narrative is one of Christians and non-Christians facing off in a culture war. Certainly strong disagreements are unavoidable at times, but the principle of God's goodness working through His people to bless unbelievers is still very much part of His plan.

LOOK UP GALATIANS 6:9-10.

To whom are we to do good? to all

> *Let us not get tired of doing good, for we will reap at the proper time if we don't give up. Therefore, as we have opportunity, let us work for the good of all, especially for those who belong to the household of faith.*
>
> Galatians 6:9-10

Notice that Joseph wasn't swallowed up by the Egyptian pagan culture, and neither did he rail against it. Instead he brought the wisdom and goodness of the one true God to a people who didn't yet know Him. We are to do the same—infiltrating the world with salt that preserves and light that shines the way. And while the good news of Jesus may, at times, put us in opposition to those who resist Him, we are called to love even those who persecute us.

PERSONAL REFLECTION: If you've grown up in a religious environment that stressed an "us versus the world" mentality, how do Joseph's story and God's covenant with Abraham help you reframe your role as a believer in the place God has you?

I want you to see this truth from Jesus' perspective. Matthew 5–7 records Jesus' Sermon on the Mount where He speaks to a handful of His disciples and a throng of people who are listening in. Here we get a taste of what it means to live as Christ-followers in His kingdom.

READ MATTHEW 5:13-16.

What two metaphors does Jesus use to describe the effect His disciples will have on the world?

*Salt of the earth.
Light of the world*

Write down everything you know about the purposes of salt and light below.

Salt: preserve, add life (spice) to food

Light: see, follow, nourish, grow

What does Jesus say will happen if we lose our saltiness?

loses its flavor - good for nothing

What specifically does Jesus say our light will bring attention to (v. 16)? (Circle the best answer below.)

(Good works)   Critical spirits   Self-righteousness   Love

As a result, to whom will the watching world give glory (v. 16)?

Father God

PERSONAL TAKE: How does the concept of being salt and light in the world differ from separating ourselves to the point of having no impact at all?

Salt; light - give life and sustenance to one another

ecclesiastical: (adj.)

1: of or relating to a church, especially as an established institution

2: suitable for use in a church[3]

When I think of salt in the American South, I think of the vast amounts we use in our foods. But salt is also used for healing wounds, cleansing bacteria, and ridding fabric of stains. Perhaps the most significant use of salt in Jesus' day was the way it was used as a preservative. Since no one had a refrigerator in the first century, salt was rubbed into meats and fish as a way of maintaining their freshness. Jesus' metaphor is clear: we're to be salt that slows down the decay of this world. John Stott puts it like this, "Christian salt has no business to remain snugly in elegant little ecclesiastical salt cellars; our place is to be rubbed into the secular community, as salt is rubbed into meat, to stop it going bad."[4]

RETURN TO TODAY'S TEXT AND READ GENESIS 41:56-57 AGAIN.

How is Joseph acting as salt in the way we just talked about?

He is preserving his faith and also caring for those around him.

LOOK BACK AT GENESIS 40:8 AND 41:16.

How did Joseph shine a light toward God in these two verses?

interpretations of dreams belong to God God, not me, will give pharaoh answers

When Jesus told His disciples in Matthew 5 about being the light of the world, He didn't tell them to go create light. He simply said, "You are the light ... " (Matt. 5:14a). (Jesus' statement is based on God being the source of light shining through His disciples, then and now.) And because you're the light, don't hide your light. How absolutely silly it would be for you to put your light under a basket. We do this when we cover up our faith or neglect to reflect Jesus in situations and conversations. Joseph could have taken the credit himself for the dreams God interpreted and hidden the light of God's power through him, but he quickly proclaimed the name and abilities of the one true God.

Jesus didn't say, "Go manufacture salt." He said, "You are the salt of the earth" (Matt. 5:13a). But just as the light can be covered up, the salt can lose its flavor, its impact. The interesting truth about salt: it's a very stable compound that doesn't break down easily. However, when salt is mixed in with other sediments and impurities, it may more easily become worthless. It seems Jesus was teaching that when we, as believers, blend in with the world, that's when we lose our saltiness— when we try to mix a little of Jesus with a little of the world.

PERSONAL RESPONSE: In what area(s) of your life are you covering up the light of Jesus? In what area(s) have you mixed your love for Jesus with your love for the world? Take some time to write about this below.

Not acknowledging my faith Volunteering, helping others

Salt and light are agents of impact. Salt and light give and expend themselves. Salt and light are distinct from their surroundings. Jesus' message is not that we as believers aren't to be separate in some way from the world. Joseph was very distinct from his pagan surroundings. Jesus' message is that our distinction as salt and light should help heal, preserve, shine, and illuminate the way for the world around us, so that others will see and glorify our Father in heaven. More simply put, we're to be separate *from* the world *for* the world.

We have the Spirit of God in us, the most valuable treasure in our storehouses and our most meaningful offering to others.

The picture of Joseph flinging open every storehouse in Egypt while the "nations" came to his door is such an earthy, tangible picture of the abundance and availability of the goodness of God. I can hardly stand it. But, of course, this epic picture is only meaningful because the storehouses Joseph flung open overflowed with grain. And the storehouses overflowed with grain because Joseph had the wisdom to store that grain while the harvest was plentiful. And Joseph had the wisdom to store that grain during the abundant years because he was surrendered to the Spirit of God.

Each of us has a storehouse we can open up to the people around us. Those storehouses and the way we open them may look differently for each of us. It may look like bringing someone into our homes, giving a generous gift, making ourselves available for a ministry or a relationship, or offering someone a job. Along with these tangible offerings, we have the Spirit of God in us, the most valuable treasure in our storehouses and our most meaningful offering to others.

PERSONAL RESPONSE: What's in your storehouse, and what is God asking you to do with it for the benefit of others and for His glory?

Money - give away
resources

DAY 4
THE FAMILY IS BACK
GENESIS 42:1-9

Is there anything more complicated than family dynamics? If they were simple, all the really good family counselors in the world would have to be really good at something else because who would need them? Our family relationships, no matter how close-knit or terribly strained, are complicated because we're intimately attached to one another and because every relationship in a family is interwoven with all the other family relationships. Nothing in a family happens in a vacuum. (And sometimes no one in your family wants to help you vacuum, and that is also a problem.)

The sons of Israel were among those who came to buy grain, for the famine was in the land of Canaan.

Genesis 42:5

I particularly love that the narrative of Joseph's story never strays far from the reality of his family. Even during his twenty years in Egypt, estranged from his brothers and father, you always have the impression that they're never far away, maybe even lurking just around the next page. It's almost as if at any moment they could bust through the front door looking for Joseph's guest room, wondering if there's any seltzer water in the fridge and if he possibly has a fresh lime to go with it because, boy, it was a long journey.

READ GENESIS 42:1-9.

What significant place had the famine reached?

Canaan

As we continue to learn new details about Joseph's story, we always want to keep significant events, places, and people that we've discussed previously in mind.

READ GENESIS 17:3-8.

PERSONAL TAKE: Based on verse 8 in particular, what seems surprising about a famine being in the land of Canaan? *God blessed it*

Returning to today's text, how severe was the famine based on Jacob's words in Genesis 42:2? *severe enough they could die*

Genesis 42:3-4 gives us insight into the family division that still plagued Jacob's household. Ten of the brothers were sent down to Egypt, but one was held back.

Who were the mothers of the ten sons who journeyed to Egypt? And who was the mother of the son who was held back? Hint: She was also Joseph's mother. (Go back to p. 18 if you need help.)

PERSONAL TAKE: Considering the family rivalries, the brothers' deception, and the favoritism Jacob still showed to Rachel's children, what do you think it would take for redemption to occur? (I'm not asking for specifics, just general principles of what you think would have to happen.) *repentance forgiveness*

Based on Jacob's words to his sons in Genesis 42:1, do they appear to have changed much over the past twenty years? Why or why not? *No, they still need instruction, feel guilty*

Dwelling with the God of promise is far superior to dwelling in the place of promise.

When the ten brothers arrived in Egypt, they didn't recognize Joseph. We know from other verses that Joseph spoke a different language, wore Egyptian attire, had a different name, and was governor over Egypt (Gen. 41:37-45; 42:23), all of which would have masked his identity. What strikes me about today's scene is that while Joseph's outward change was significant, it was the sanctifying work we know God had done in his heart that was the most miraculous transformation.

And yet, how little seems to have changed about the brothers. Even though they'd been living in the promised land of Canaan, their hearts don't appear to have softened much, despite them having access to the God of their fathers. On the other hand, though Joseph had been living outside the land, he'd been dwelling in the presence of God. And dwelling with the God of promise is far superior to dwelling in the place of promise.

PERSONAL REFLECTION: Maybe you feel like you're not in the "place of promise" right now. In what ways can you submit to the God of promise, who has the power to change you from the inside out? *focus on Him, spend time w/ Him*

Dear friends, I can't tell you how significant this truth has been to me. You may be waiting for a difficult circumstance to change, but with Jesus in that place with you, the greater miracle is that you can be changed. Keep seeking the God of promise and leave the place of promise in His hands.

In reference to this thought, my friend Emily said, "The overarching truth here is God's presence is the promise in every situation. Our physical location doesn't determine our redemption story; He is our redemption story. So although some circumstances remain unchanging, our God remains, too. The gift of Himself is the fulfillment of the promise. As we dwell in His presence, we experience life change whether we're in Egypt or Canaan. Forgiveness, hope, redemption, and reconciliation can and will occur because He is with us. Circumstances do not achieve this. He does."

Speaking of promises, when the brothers bowed before Joseph, what did Joseph remember (Gen. 42:9)? his dreams

The dream God gave Joseph symbolized all the brothers bowing down to Joseph. Who was missing at this point? Benjamin

The experience of seeing his brothers fall to the ground before him resembled his dream closely enough for it to come rushing back to the forefront of Joseph's mind. But this scene wasn't the fulfillment of the dream because not all the brothers were present. However, this experience served as a powerful reminder to Joseph that God was still at work, that He hadn't forgotten Joseph, and that God was going to do what He said He would do.

Turn back to the meaning of Manasseh's name in Genesis 41:51. How is this description different than what happened to Joseph in Genesis 42:9? He did not forget his father's house

Scholar K. A. Mathews describes the situation this way, "Despite [Joseph's] zeal to 'forget' his difficult past, he cannot escape it. It is facing his painful past that leads the way to his deliverance from the past."[5] Regardless of what exactly Joseph meant by forgetting his family when Manasseh was born, he couldn't have possibly imagined the scene that was taking place before him.

I don't know how you answered the "personal take" about what would be necessary for redemption to transpire between Joseph and his brothers, but I imagine forgiveness was one of your answers. The return of the brothers in today's text may have brought up some painful memories for you, memories of betrayal and hurt. Whether the people

who have hurt you are still alive or whether you see them often or not at all, my prayer is for you to offer forgiveness and find freedom as we continue to follow Joseph's story.

PERSONAL RESPONSE: Is there anyone from your past you haven't forgiven but know you need to? Take some time to put this before the Lord and ask Him to lead you in forgiving that person.

Sometimes He wants to bring healing and reconciliation to something that's still broken, and this healing work may require an encounter with our pasts.

Sometimes it's wise to "forget" certain parts of our pasts, never again to look back. This is especially true if you and the Lord have already dealt with past times of darkness or sin. I'm a big believer in not revisiting what God has taken great pains to deliver us from. That said, other times we can be guilty of running from that which God wants to redeem. Sometimes He wants to bring healing and reconciliation to something that's still broken, and this healing work may require an encounter with our pasts.

I know what you're thinking, *how do I know which is which?* The first answer is that the Holy Spirit, God's Word, and the counsel of trusted believers will help you discern the difference. The second answer is that if you can see hearts softening to the redemptive work of Christ and if there's an opportunity for further forgiveness and restoration, God may be calling you to face something from your past so He can redeem it. In my experience, the Lord has never asked me to do this until He's changed me enough to face my past from a different place, as a different woman—all because of His sanctifying work in my life. I pray the Lord will give you further insight as we will see the firm boundaries Joseph set and how carefully he handled his brothers in the coming pages.

LET'S CLOSE WITH A NEW TESTAMENT REMINDER OF GOD'S REDEMPTIVE POWER AS WRITTEN IN HEBREWS 12:12-15.

PERSONAL RESPONSE: If the Lord is speaking to you from today's study, write a response below.

DAY 5
A CAUTIOUS REUNION
GENESIS 42:10-20

We ended yesterday's study by focusing on forgiveness, especially as it relates to people from our pasts. Forgiveness is essential to a relationship with Jesus Christ. In Matthew's Gospel, Jesus says that if we don't forgive others their sins, our Father won't forgive us our sins (Matt. 6:15). Forgiveness is that central. When we experience Jesus' astounding and inexhaustible forgiveness, we will want to forgive others, even if for a time we squirm and struggle through the process.

When we experience Jesus' astounding and inexhaustible forgiveness, we will want to forgive others, even if for a time we squirm and struggle through the process.

That said, sometimes we confuse forgiveness with restored relationship. While forgiveness can lead to restoration, forgiveness doesn't require it. In addition, forgiveness isn't synonymous with suddenly having to be best friends with an abusive ex-boyfriend or letting a wildly unhealthy person back into our lives as the boss. Over the next few chapters we'll get a clearer picture of what forgiveness is and what it isn't. Some of us will be convicted to forgive because our hearts have grown bitter and hard; others of us will realize we've confused forgiveness with allowing ourselves to be trampled on by an ex-offender all over again. My prayer is for none of us to stop short of forgiving fully from the heart. I pray we also don't turn forgiveness into something God never intended it to be.

READ GENESIS 42:7-22. WE'RE READING A FEW VERSES FROM YESTERDAY TO GAIN CONTEXT.

How did Joseph speak to his brothers when seeing them for the first time in twenty years? (Circle your answer below.)

Tenderly   Harshly   Religiously   Amiably

TRUE/FALSE: *Joseph treated his brothers like family (Gen. 42:7).*   F

PERSONAL TAKE: When Joseph first noticed that his brother Benjamin was missing, what might he have thought happened to Benjamin based on his own experience?

After Joseph asked his brothers where they had come from, a series of short exchanges followed, each one revealing important information. In the section below, detail what Joseph discovered from his brothers through each exchange.

JOSEPH	TEN BROTHERS
v. 7: Where do you come from?	v. 7: From _____ to buy _____
v. 9: You are spies!	v. 11: We are all sons of one _____. We are 12 _____.
v. 12: You've come to see the weakness of the land.	v. 13: We were _12_ brothers. The _youngest_ is now with our father. One is no longer _____.

PERSONAL TAKE: Out of the information Joseph has gleaned about his family so far, what do you think was most significant to him? Why?

Jacob, Benjamin

How did Joseph's scheme give him the best shot at seeing his only full-brother, Benjamin, again and most likely his father, Jacob?

While Joseph knew his brothers weren't spies and were clearly in Egypt to buy grain, what he didn't know was whether their hearts had changed. By accusing them of being spies who had come to see the areas of weakness in Egypt, Joseph was drawing the thoughts and intents of their hearts toward the surface. Had they done the same thing to Benjamin that they had done to him? Would they leave one brother to die in prison? Were they still deceitful and ruthless? Joseph was going to find out by devising a plan to test their integrity. Nine of them would be imprisoned, and one would be released to retrieve Benjamin.

After holding the ten brothers in prison for three days, how did Joseph significantly alter his plan (vv. 18-20)? let them go, except 1

On the third day, who did Joseph say he feared/revered? god

PERSONAL TAKE: Why do you think Joseph changed his plan during that three-day period?

We're not told why Joseph changed his plan from detaining nine brothers and releasing one to releasing nine and detaining one. Certainly nine brothers would be able to carry a lot more grain back to Jacob and Benjamin than one brother could carry, so that might have influenced Joseph's decision. Or perhaps the Holy Spirit spoke to Joseph, assuring him that retaining one brother would be enough to accomplish what God had in mind. We simply don't know, but I personally believe that while God was working on Joseph's brothers in prison, He was also working in Joseph's heart.

PERSONAL REFLECTION: When faced with an emotionally-charged situation, how has stepping back for a few days helped you gain perspective and hear God's voice?

Most scholars see Joseph's initially harsh actions toward his brothers as redemptive, not condemning. While he puts them through the ringer, scholar K. A. Mathews says, "This charge was a means of determining the character of his brothers, not personal retaliation."[6] I trust Joseph's heart while testing his brothers because the Lord had so thoroughly tested Joseph. Similarly, we can only be trusted to speak into the lives of others when our own character has been tested.

It reminds me of Jesus' words in Matthew 7:3-5,

> Why do you look at the splinter in your brother's eye but don't notice the beam of wood in your own eye? Or how can you say to your brother, "Let me take the splinter out of your eye," and look, there's a beam of wood in your own eye? Hypocrite! First take the beam of wood out of your eye, and then you will see clearly to take the splinter out of your brother's eye.

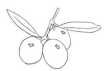

Brothers and sisters, if someone is overtaken in any wrongdoing, you who are spiritual, restore such a person with a gentle spirit, watching out for yourselves so that you also won't be tempted.

Galatians 6:1

I think we can all agree that if Joseph had entered Egypt with anything in his eye, the Lord had removed it during a remarkably thorough process of sanctification.

While I think of the brothers as beam-people and Joseph as more of a speck sort of guy, the principle remains. Joseph had surrendered himself to the Lord, and now he could be trusted to shepherd the hearts of his brothers.

READ GALATIANS 6:1.

What is our disposition supposed to be when confronting someone?

Gentleness

What are we supposed to do to make sure we're not tempted in the process?

consider ourselves lest

PERSONAL RESPONSE: If you're needing to confront someone who has wronged you or another person, what steps can you take to make sure you're doing it with a humble and loving spirit?

You may have to draw firm boundaries; you may have to show tough love; and you may have to see whether or not a loved one passes a test of integrity before entrusting them with more of your heart. This is wisdom. But, we can never compromise gentleness, humility, or love.

We've seen a different side of Joseph this week. While his actions have appeared harsh, I believe he knew that unless his brothers dealt with the sin they'd committed against him they would never be free. I also believe that by remembering the dreams God had given him, Joseph was compelled to press toward their complete fulfillment. By dealing firmly with his brothers, Joseph would hopefully draw both Benjamin and his beloved father into his presence in the near future. Again, Dr. Sailhamer says it best: "What awaited the brothers was not the 'evil' they intended for Joseph but the 'good' God intended for them through Joseph."[7]

NOTES

SESSION 4 VIEWER GUIDE

FAITHFUL IN ABUNDANCE

GROUP DISCUSSION

What portion of the video teaching really resonated with you? Why?

If it's true that we won't serve God more in the good times than we're willing to serve Him in the difficult ones, how does this encourage you to be faithful wherever God has you right now?

Though Pharaoh seemingly had it all, Joseph had the one thing that Pharaoh didn't possess: the Holy Spirit. How is the Holy Spirit in you your most profound gift to the world?

Joseph influenced Pharaoh to bring about significant change. How are you leveraging your gift of influence for eternal purposes?

When you minister out of your abundance to someone going through a difficult time, how does it tangibly remind you of God's abundance toward you?

How can you be a storehouse for others? What do you have to give (time, resources, money, relationship, space)? Explain.

To access the video teaching sessions, use the instructions in the back of your Bible study book.

Shrimp and Grits (serves 4–6)

INGREDIENTS

Grits:

3½ cups chicken stock (plus more, if needed)

4 tablespoons butter

½ cup heavy cream

1 clove garlic, minced

1 cup grits

Salt and black pepper, to taste

Shrimp:

⅓ cup butter

½ cup chopped shallots

1 large clove garlic, minced

2 pounds uncooked, peeled, deveined shrimp

½ cup chicken stock

4 tomatoes, diced

½ cup prosciutto, cut into thin strips

1 cup andouille sausage, cubed

¼ cup chopped parsley

¼ cup chopped chives

DIRECTIONS

In a large stockpot over medium heat, combine chicken stock, butter, heavy cream, and garlic. Bring to a boil. Gradually add the grits, whisking constantly. Reduce heat to low and simmer uncovered until grits thicken. Add salt and pepper to taste.

At the same time, melt ⅓ cup of butter in a large skillet over medium heat. Add shallots and garlic, sautéing until tender. Add shrimp and cook for about 2 minutes or until shrimp are pink. Set shrimp aside. Add chicken stock to the skillet and boil for about 6 minutes. Add tomatoes, prosciutto, and sausage. Cook for 2 minutes. Then return the shrimp to the skillet along with the parsley and chives, cooking until warm through.

Spoon grits into shallow bowls, and top with shrimp mixture.

Sometimes you need comfort food. Nothing says comfort quite like shrimp and grits. It's another Southern favorite, perfect for dinner or a Bible study gathering. You'll be the most popular person in the room—in a really humble sort of way.

EXTRAVAGANT MERCY

I planned to serve my friends a Bolognese sauce over pasta for dinner. Simple enough. I had the sauce simmering on the stove in one pot while I boiled the water for the rigatoni in another. Then in walked my friend with her box of gluten-free, red lentil fusilli—because, why be fun when you can be boring and healthy? I added an additional saucepan to the stovetop for the fake fusilli. Another dear soul trotted into my kitchen hankering for something entirely different, something with more protein, like quinoa. Onto the stove went pot number four, producing a perfectly bubbling quartet. When my last guest breezed in asking for steamed vegetables, I kindly and very loudly articulated, "I don't have enough saucepans for all you people and your tastes!" (The truth is I barely have enough for my own some days.)

I've been thinking a lot about the ways our modern world allows us to curate our lives down to our specific dietary desires, the firmness of our mattresses, and the types of cream in our coffee—plain, hazelnut, french vanilla, organic. We're used to being able to customize our experiences to our exact liking. But I've discovered that being able to customize something is not the same as being able to control it. We're still subject to all the things we can't or don't know how to tame, no matter how tailored our environments.

Last week we left Joseph at the height of success and power—second-in-command to Pharaoh and overseer of all of Egypt. I imagine Joseph's position afforded him a variety of customizable luxuries. Yet this week's Scripture passage reveals that despite Joseph's exceptional power, he still had no control over his father and brothers. Joseph could steer his brothers in the right direction, but he couldn't change their hearts. He could attempt to draw his father out of Canaan, but he couldn't force Jacob out. The big things, the eternal things lay in the Lord's hands.

As much as I might think I'm managing my world by honing my preferences, the truth is I'm fully dependent upon the Lord for everything that really matters to me. This includes the lives of my beloved family and friends, the health of those I pray for, the direction of my ministry, and even my own breath. Joseph's hope hung firmly on the God of the universe. It wasn't flimsily hooked to an illusion of control. God honors such hope, both yesterday and today.

DAY 1
SEVERE MERCY
GENESIS 42:21-35

This week we'll be following God's redemptive plan for Jacob's family in the midst of profound brokenness. Jacob's favoritism of Joseph, the guilt of the brothers, and Joseph's own pain from what they'd done to him would coalesce into a sea of complex turmoil that would look perfectly insurmountable. The very good news is God's hand is able to tame any sea, even the relational kind. Only He can humble tumultuous waves into a glassy surface so smooth it will reflect His glory and His alone.

For those of you who find yourselves in difficult family relationships, I pray God will give you hope over the next few weeks as we watch Him restore what appears to be irreconcilably broken. To be clear, we're not heading toward a Disney® version of everyone living happily ever after in Joseph's castle. (Although I do love a good fairy-tale ending, and I've always wondered what it'd be like to have a butler). Our destination is much better. We'll witness God and His covenant with Abraham pressing forward through Jacob's family, consuming every good and bad human action along the way as fuel for His plan of redemption.

No matter the brokenness of your family, no matter how strained those relationships, God is able to bless, hold, and strengthen you. He's also able to accomplish His redemptive plan through you, not just in spite of your suffering, but often because of it (Gen. 49:22-26).

READ GENESIS 42:18-26. I'M HAVING YOU REREAD A FEW VERSES FROM LAST WEEK TO REFRESH YOUR MEMORY.

What new information do you discover about Joseph's reaction to his brothers when they threw him in the pit (v. 21)?

plead w/ them

How did the brothers interpret the trouble they were experiencing in Egypt (vv. 21-22)? *as punishment*

No matter the brokenness of your family, no matter how strained those relationships, God is able to bless, hold, and strengthen you.

PERSONAL TAKE: When bad things happen to you, how do you typically interpret them? Do you see them as judgment from God for some sin you've committed? *Sometimes*

The brothers made a connection between their present difficult situation and their past sin against Joseph. "*Obviously*, we are being punished for what we did to our brother," they concluded (v. 21a, *emphasis mine*). (Your translation may say, "surely," "truly," or "in truth.") The brothers clearly saw that their actions deserved a consequence and implied that God was bringing judgment against them. It's also interesting that when the brothers talked about their punishment, they used the Hebrew word *'ašam*, which "refers both to guilt and to its punishment. The two are inseparable." Their statement could be translated, "we are guilty and being punished."[1]

> One important note before we go further: Jesus made clear that we're not to automatically interpret the difficulties and suffering in our lives as God's punishment. When Jesus restored the sight of a man who was born blind His disciples asked Him: "Rabbi, who sinned, this man or his parents, that he was born blind?" Jesus definitively answered, "Neither … " (John 9:2-3).
>
> There's a big difference between automatically viewing our suffering as God's punishment on us and recognizing His restorative discipline, which can sometimes be painful. (See Heb. 12:7-13 for a helpful passage on this topic.) Keep this contrast in mind as we move forward.

While we may think it obvious for the brothers to make a connection between their current circumstances and past sin, we as human beings don't always recognize God's discipline in our lives. **Sometimes we don't even recognize our own sin.**

According to Genesis 3:5, who is the source of the knowledge of good and evil? God

According to the prophecy of Jeremiah 31:33, how do we know God's teaching about all things, including right and wrong?
Written on our heart

"Instead, this is the covenant I will make with the house of Israel after those days"—the LORD's declaration. "I will put my teaching within them and write it on their hearts. I will be their God, and they will be my people."

Jeremiah 31:33

PERSONAL TAKE: Why should we consider the brothers' recognition of their sin a blessing from God? Give this some thought and record your answer below. *To repent and turn towards god*

While we don't usually view conviction of sin as a gift, that's exactly what it is. The real tragedy isn't experiencing guilt because of our sin, it's being in sin and not knowing it or suppressing our knowledge of it (Rom. 1:18). Only when we see our sin and confess it can we receive forgiveness. The very fact that the brothers were beginning to acknowledge that what they had done to Joseph was horribly wrong was a blessing in itself.

PERSONAL RESPONSE: Is anyone in your life caught in a dark place of sin they're not aware of or a place they are refusing to acknowledge? Romans 2:4b, one of my favorite verses, says, "God's kindness is intended to lead you to repentance." Take some time to pray for this person. Pray for his or her awareness of sin and need for Christ's redemption. Pray for God's kindness to lead him or her to repentance.

Describe Joseph's reaction when he overheard his brothers talking about what they'd done to him (Gen. 42:24). He wept

PERSONAL TAKE: Genesis 42:24 is the first of several times the Scripture records Joseph weeping (Gen. 43:30; 45:2,14-15; 46:29; 50:1). What does this tell you about his heart? *It was broken - he missed his family*

After Joseph gained his composure, he had Simeon bound before his brothers' eyes. Simeon was the second oldest of the brothers. It's possible Joseph was planning to imprison the firstborn, Reuben, but when he overheard Reuben talking about how he had tried to save Joseph, perhaps Joseph was moved and went for the next brother in line.

If the brothers cared anything about Simeon, which remained to be seen, they'd have to come back with Benjamin for Simeon's release. Even if they didn't care about Simeon, Joseph knew the famine would outlast the grain his brothers were returning home with, so they'd have to come back no matter what. This arrangement ensured that Benjamin would also be brought back with them. Brilliant, if you ask me.

Remember from last week, it was precisely when Joseph remembered his dreams that he began to accuse his brothers of being spies (Gen. 42:9). Rather than interpreting Joseph's harsh demeanor as an angry response to those who had hurt him, it could be that he was trying to work in accordance with the dreams God had given him—dreams that were predicated on his family being together. Now that Joseph remembered what God promised him, he worked out a plan in step with that vision.

PERSONAL REFLECTION: There's a difference between working in accordance with God's plan and frantically trying to "save" His plan. Is there any area in your life where you're trying to manipulate or control an outcome on your own terms? If so, describe how you can wait on the Lord while still working with Him on His terms. *Eyes*

If severe mercy is what it takes to rescue me from my waywardness, I'll take it any day over the kind of mercy that's too soft for the task.

READ GENESIS 42:27-35.

When the brothers found their silver in their sacks they were terrified because it looked as if they'd stolen the grain. How would they explain this to the harsh Egyptian lord (Joseph) when they returned to Egypt to retrieve Simeon? Joseph having the silver returned to the brothers at first appeared to be a generous gift, but the infinitely more valuable gift was how God would use it to further convict their hearts—conviction that would hopefully lead them to repentance.

Look closely at verse 28. Who did the brothers conclude was behind this terrifying turn of events? God

We can't miss this—behind the brothers' punishment was God's redemptive mercy! God would use something as severe as a famine, Simeon's imprisonment, and a "harsh Egyptian ruler" to woo the brothers back to Himself and ultimately back to a place of provision that would save their lives.

I remember many years ago when God used the severe mercy of the loss of a few treasured friendships, a lost record deal, and a dark time of uncertainty to rescue me back to Himself. I have cried many times out of pure gratefulness for God's tough and relentless love that deals with my sin and disciplines me when I stray from Him. If severe mercy is what it takes to rescue me from my waywardness, I'll take it any day over the kind of mercy that's too soft for the task.

Is God using severe mercy in your life to get your attention? What I love about His character is that the discipline God brings is always for our good and always borne out of love. Since the gift of God's Son, Jesus, we don't have to live under condemnation or a sense of dread. A passage in Acts points to the freedom we have when we repent (turn from our sinful direction and back to the Lord).

READ ACTS 3:19-20.

PERSONAL REFLECTION: Do you need to repent? Confess your sin to the Lord, talk to a trusted believer if you feel stuck in a certain pattern, receive the forgiveness of Jesus, and let times of refreshing come. *Yes*

If you're going through a time of discipline, remember these words from Hebrews 12:6a, "the Lord disciplines the one he loves." I find myself smiling as I write these words, smiling at you, as if you're sitting right here in front of me. God only brings correction and discipline to those He dearly loves—for it is then that our eyes are opened to the sin that destroys us, our hearts opened to the forgiveness that heals us, and our hands opened to the times of refreshment that are on their way.

DAY 2
WAITING AND TRUSTING

GENESIS 42:36–43:14

This may come as little surprise, but cell service is hard to come by in the Amazon jungle. It's not beneath me to beg God for a sliver of a signal whilst balancing on top of our hammock boat, phone pressed to the sky. Amazonians pass me by in their canoes, inquisitively staring at me like I really do need to get a life and try things like fishing, gardening, sunset watching, and in-person conversations. Being tethered to technology has its conveniences, but it can also be a burden.

One year on my way to JMI's Annual Jungle Pastor's Conference, the Holy Spirit prompted me to head this technology distraction off at the pass by turning my phone off for the week. I knew He wanted me to be fully present with Him and His people, not chasing cell service. However, I was leaving a lot of unresolved work problems back home, and I wasn't sure how they would be handled without me. Frankly, I felt very essential to myself. At the same time I also sensed the Lord inviting me to trust that He could work these things out without me. Why do I always feel like this concept is breaking news? With the press of a button my phone powered down and my soul leaned in. I was in for a good week.

The day after I returned home from the Amazon, I met someone who would turn out to be an answer to prayer and a solution to many of the difficult issues I had been dealing with. Peace was restored. Most surprising, the Lord didn't even need me to pull it off.

As we make our way through Joseph's story, I'm continually impressed by God's providential hand accomplishing His work regardless of what all the people in our story choose to do or not do. Jacob and his sons were still free to make decisions and choices, but God in His incomprehensible sovereignty never lost control. While Joseph and Simeon were in Egypt and the rest of the brothers and their father were all the way back in Canaan, God was fulfilling His promises. And Joseph wouldn't need a phone to help make it happen.

READ GENESIS 42:36–43:14.

According to Genesis 43:7, which two people did Joseph keep asking his brothers about, and why are they significant to the fulfillment of Joseph's dreams? (Look back at Gen. 37:6-10 if you need to refresh your memory.)

When our hopes are up they have farther to fall, which is why we sometimes find it easier to give up on a dream altogether rather than keep waiting on God to fulfill His promises.

Theoretically, Joseph should have known without a doubt that both Jacob and Benjamin were still alive since both were essential to the fulfillment of his dreams. However, more than twenty years had gone by and Joseph had made an entirely new life apart from his family and Hebrew culture. I wonder if he struggled with his faith the way I sometimes do, sincerely believing certain promises of God while simultaneously thinking, *there's no way.*

Once Joseph realized his father and brother were alive, his desire to see them must have intensified. The dream was closer than ever to being fulfilled and hope in God's promises was renewed, but his angst must have increased too. When our hopes are up they have farther to fall, which is why we sometimes find it easier to give up on a dream altogether rather than keep waiting on God to fulfill His promises.

PERSONAL TAKE: Joseph now knew that Benjamin and Jacob were indeed alive, yet his brothers were gone and all he could do was continue to work while he waited. Describe what you think it was like for him as he waited for God to reunite him with his family. *Stressful, anxious*

LOOK BACK AT GENESIS 42:36-38.

Back in Canaan, what did Jacob immediately refuse to let his sons do when discussing a return trip to Egypt? *take Benjamin*

Jacob has further alienated all but Rachel's sons by essentially saying Joseph and Benjamin were his only true sons. How was Jacob's sin of favoritism—we could possibly say idolatry—working against him right then and against God's redemptive plan?

I suppose it was a good thing that Joseph didn't know all the conversations his father and brothers were having, the ones we've been privy to in today's reading. They probably would have only made him worry. The future of Israel seemed to be resting on the woe-is-me shoulders of Jacob and on the equally unstable shoulders of Reuben and Judah (Gen. 43:3-10).

And she conceived again, gave birth to a son, and said, "This time I will praise the LORD." Therefore she named him Judah. Then Leah stopped having children.

Genesis 29:35

PERSONAL REFLECTION: When was the last time you felt like God's plan for your life was hinging on frail and broken people? How does Joseph's story so far remind you that God is sovereign and working all things together to accomplish His plan, regardless of how humans choose to respond?

Describe the differences between Reuben's and Judah's offers of help should Benjamin not return safely to their father. (See Gen. 42:37; 43:8-9.)

Reuben - sons
Judah - self, becer name

PERSONAL TAKE: Which appears to be the more selfless offer, and why?

Reuben

Though the change is subtle, Judah was beginning to emerge as the leader of his brothers. His rise to leadership would become increasingly important. You'll recall from Session 2 that Judah was the fourth child born to Leah and Jacob. In the coming days Judah will gain a more significant place in our story, and I'm looking forward to watching this unfold with you.

IN THE MEANTIME, LOOK BACK AT GENESIS 29:35.

What did Leah say after giving birth to Judah? Why do you think this is significant? I will praise the Lord

I don't want us to get ahead of ourselves, but it seems to me at Judah's birth we get a hint that God has significant plans for his life.

READ GENESIS 37:25.

What were the Ishmaelites carrying with them on their camels? How does their cargo inventory compare to the one in Genesis 43:11? List the similarities.

Spices,
how it is grain food

I've always found it fascinating that some of the goods Joseph must have seen, smelled, and maybe even tasted on his way down to Egypt were the very gifts his father and brothers would send him as a peace offering more than twenty years later. Jacob hoped these gifts as well as the returned silver would appease this harsh "lord of Egypt" and prompt him to show mercy to Jacob's family.

We began today's lesson with Jacob's resistance to his sons returning to Egypt with Benjamin. What changed his mind?

According to Genesis 43:14, what did Jacob specifically call God?

God Almighty

What did Jacob hope God would grant his sons? mercy

The name, God Almighty, was the name given in relation to the covenant promise God made with Abraham in Genesis 17. I believe Jacob used that name as a way of appealing to that promise, the promise of God to make Abraham into the father of many nations. For the promise to be fulfilled, Jacob's family line would have to survive. And for Jacob's descendants to survive, God would have to show mercy to the family. (I hope you will watch this week's teaching video because we're going to look at this word *mercy* and note how Genesis 43:14 is the first time the word is used in the Bible. You won't want to miss it.)

While recently reading Psalm 33 as part of my daily Bible reading plan, I thought of Joseph being in a position to put his trust in God instead of in people or circumstances.

READ PSALM 33:13-22.

From where does salvation not come (vv. 16-17)?

Man's Strength

Our hope and our strength aren't found in a person.

The psalmist reminds us that our hope and our strength aren't found in a person. The salvation of Jacob's family didn't rest on Pharaoh, Jacob, Jacob's sons, or even on Joseph. The Lord is the One who rescues from death and, as specifically mentioned in this psalm, famine. Without God's sovereign hand working out His plan, each person's agenda would have failed, including Joseph's.

Surely Joseph wondered if his brothers would ever make it back to Egypt and whether Benjamin would be with them. He probably wondered if his elderly father would ever leave Canaan and come to reside in Egypt. He may have worried that some of his family might not make it through the long journey during a famine. Regardless of Joseph's perspective, it seemed his dreams were hanging in the balance, determined by the decisions of Joseph's brothers and father, people who were hundreds of miles away. But this couldn't be further from the truth. These life-changing details rested in God's hands.

IN CLOSING, READ 1 PETER 5:6-7.

Throughout today's study we've thought about Joseph having to wait and trust while his father and brothers were back home in Canaan discussing and preparing to return to Egypt. Details were emerging. A larger plan was unfolding. In light of this, respond to one of the two closing responses, whichever most closely fits your current situation.

PERSONAL RESPONSE: What are you losing sleep over because you're trying to control it but can't? What do you feel continually anxious about? Take some time with the Lord and entrust this situation to His care and sovereignty.

PERSONAL RESPONSE: If you're not anxious but you're simply contemplating all that you're waiting for, my question for you is—how are you waiting? What's your posture? Which of God's promises are you trusting? How are you living in expectation (Ps. 5:3)? Explain.

We wait for the LORD; He is our help and shield. For our hearts rejoice in him because we trust in his holy name. May your faithful love rest on us, LORD, for we put our hope in you.

PSALM 33:20-22

DAY 3
AN UNSHAKABLE DREAM
GENESIS 43:15-26

We're well past the halfway point in our study on the life of Joseph. I want to encourage you to keep going. Starting something is easy but finishing it requires commitment and fortitude. The fact that you've made it this far tells me without a doubt you can finish this study strong. Keep setting aside the time for each day's work, and don't worry when you get behind. Catch up when you can. Joseph's story in particular builds upon itself, and you'll find the reward at the end is greater than the sum of its parts.

Yesterday we left Jacob in Canaan, Joseph and Simeon in Egypt, and the rest of Jacob's sons, including Benjamin, about to embark on a journey from Canaan to Egypt. The famine was severe. Jacob was afraid. The brothers' relationships were fractured. Joseph was presumably waiting with faithful anticipation—and possibly doubt, if he's anything like me. Despite the uncertainty and frailty of our trials and humanity, the hook upon which we can hang all our hope is God's character—He is good and in full control. We'll continue to see this truth unfold today.

READ GENESIS 43:15-22.

What specifically prompted Joseph to tell his steward to go prepare a meal at his house for his family?

Despite the uncertainty and frailty of our trials and humanity, the hook upon which we can hang all our hope is God's character—He is good and in full control.

Verse 18 tells us the brothers were afraid when they found out they were being taken to Joseph's house. We know from Egyptian history that men in Joseph's position commonly had holding cells within their homes, so this possibility probably added to their fear.[2]

What specifically were the brothers afraid would happen to them? Write down their laundry list from verse 18. make slaves, take donkeys

PERSONAL REFLECTION: Do you tend to anticipate problems and worst-case scenarios before they even happen? Explain. yes

Scholars believe that part of Joseph's reason for testing his brothers was to determine if their character had changed and if they'd turned into honest men.[3] So far, they seemed to be passing the test. They told Joseph they had a brother who was still alive and that they'd bring him to Joseph, and they did so. They returned the silver they found in their sacks and brought additional silver for a new round of grain. Even though Joseph still didn't have a lot to go on, at least he knew they hadn't done to Benjamin what they'd done to him and that they seemed genuinely concerned about returning the silver.

I have to believe the brothers' long list of fears about what they thought was going to happen to them stemmed directly from what they'd done to Joseph and the guilt they'd never dealt with. This is especially true since we learned on Day 1 of this week that they equated the returned silver with God's punishment (Gen. 42:28).

I resonate with the brothers' terror. Especially in my younger years, I lived in constant fear that God's punishment was either nipping at my heels or right around the corner about to pounce on me. I lived with guilt, some that I shouldn't have carried and some that was rightly mine—I didn't know what to do with either one. Whenever I read about the way the brothers interpreted every good or bad thing that happened to them as the just reward their sin, I think about the mercy and grace of God that freed me from guilt as a way of life. **If your view of God is continually punitive, freedom awaits you in the person of Jesus.**

PERSONAL REFLECTION: Are you living in fear of punishment because of a past sin (or sins) that you've never dealt with? Describe. *Yes*

Look up 1 John 1:8-9. How are we cleansed from past and present unrighteousness?

Look up 1 John 2:1-2. Who is our Advocate before the Father when we sin? Jesus

PERSONAL RESPONSE: How do these passages help you think biblically about your sin and God's remedy for it?

I didn't want to miss an opportunity for us to see Jesus' sacrifice as the means of our cleansing and forgiveness. You can walk in freedom. You no longer have to live in fear like Joseph's brothers (1 John 4:18). Let's return to our story in Genesis.

READ GENESIS 43:23-26.

To the brothers' utter shock, how did Joseph's steward respond to them in verse 23? Do not be afraid - Your God God of your father

To whom did Joseph's Egyptian steward attribute the brothers' returned silver? God

God was the brothers' Advocate here even though they were guilty—not of stealing the silver but of much worse, selling their brother. Are we seeing a foreshadowing of Jesus Christ as our ultimate Advocate before the Father?

And it gets even better. We miss this in our English translations, but in verse 23 when the steward told the brothers, "Don't be afraid" he also said, *šalôm*, or "Peace to you."[4] Verse 23 is so powerful because it shows us a group of clearly guilty, undeserving men go from overwhelming fear to incomprehensible peace. Only God could have caused this impossible transition. Incredible.

PERSONAL REFLECTION: Write about a time when God brought you from a place of fear to one of peace. How did He do it? What did you learn? It's good for us to write these reminders down for future remembrance.
David in hospital

I can't imagine what the brothers thought when Joseph's attendant, instead of throwing them in prison, showed them extensive hospitality: water for their feet and feed for their donkeys. I mean, it's one thing to cut them some slack, but let's not go overboard here! Or am I the only one thinking that cynically? This hospitality is God's unthinkable kindness in one of its earliest revealed forms in Scripture.

When compared with Genesis 37:20, what makes Genesis 43:26 so significant? Describe below.

No one on earth can shatter a dream whose source is in God.

I love this part of Joseph's story so much. It reminds me of an unshakable truth for those of us who are sons and daughters of the one true God: No one on earth can shatter a dream whose source is in God. As much as the brothers thought they could destroy Joseph and therefore destroy his dreams, God was the Author and Fulfiller of those dreams. The brothers were no match for the God of Abraham, Isaac, and Jacob. Today we've witnessed eleven brothers bowing down to Joseph, the fulfillment of Joseph's first dream.

PERSONAL TAKE: More than twenty years have passed since God gave Joseph the dream of his brothers bowing down to him. How do you think Joseph was now ready for the tasks ahead in a way he wasn't when he was seventeen?

PERSONAL RESPONSE: Today's study is so rich with God's providence, mercy, kindness, and faithfulness that I don't even want to try to direct your closing Personal Response. Respond to the Lord however the Holy Spirit is moving you. *Thankful, faithful, abundantly gracious and kind.*

DAY 4
A LAVISH MEAL
GENESIS 43:27-34

I hope this week has been encouraging to you as we've watched God fulfill His promise to Joseph. Though we tend to think of this as Joseph's story, it's far more accurately God's story. I used to go to Scripture looking for all the ways I could make it about me. While God's Word is certainly for us, and He loves us more than we can possibly know, I've discovered the Bible is much more compelling when we understand the story God is writing and get involved with His story, instead of trying to extract whatever tidbit applies to us. Following Christ has been the greatest joy of my life, and oddly enough, the more I'm concerned with His work and His renown, the more fulfilled I am. Who would have imagined that outcome?

The Bible is much more compelling when we understand the story God is writing and get involved with His story, instead of trying to extract whatever tidbit applies to us.

Today, we'll continue to keep our eyes on the overarching story God is writing, even as we look at the finer details. As we start our reading, let's pick up one verse from yesterday to set the larger context.

READ GENESIS 43:26-30.

Verses 29-30 describe Joseph weeping again. What caused him to weep here? He seeing for Benj. and family

Benjamin was born before Joseph was sold and sent to Egypt. We can only imagine how dear his baby brother was to Joseph, especially since they were the only two who shared Rachel as their mother. When Joseph saw Benjamin, now as a young man, Joseph was overwhelmed with emotion. Add to that the news that his father was still alive despite the famine, the gift of food he received from his family that would have reminded him of his childhood days in Canaan, and the fulfillment of his first dream when all his brothers bowed down to him—it was all too much.

In fact, the literal translation of the words "overcome by emotion" in verse 30 is Joseph's "compassion grew hot."[5] All he could do was run out of the room so his tears could flow freely. I love how scholar Bruce K. Waltke describes it, "Underneath the cloak of Egyptian appearance, his love for his family throbs."[6]

PERSONAL REFLECTION: You may have pain stemming from a family member or loved one. How does Joseph's example encourage you that, by God's grace, deep love for that person is still possible? (We'll treat this more specifically in days to come. Note that deep love doesn't necessarily mean being best friends or even being in relationship with a person. It's about the condition of your heart toward them.)

CLOSE OUT THE CHAPTER BY READING GENESIS 43:31-34.

TRUE/FALSE: *The Egyptians ate with the Hebrews because they found sharing a meal together to be an enriching cultural experience.*

We haven't yet discussed what it was like for Joseph not only to live in a foreign land with foreign customs and pagan gods but also in a land in which his culture was detested. Even though Joseph's wisdom and oversight were revered at this time, it seems he was a victim of prejudice and racism in his early days in Egypt. Many years later when God delivered the Israelites out of Egypt, He spoke to His people numerous times about treating foreigners with kindness and generosity.

Deuteronomy 24:19-22 says,

> When you reap the harvest in your field, and you forget a sheaf in the field, do not go back to get it. It is to be left for the resident alien, the fatherless, and the widow, so that the LORD your God may bless you in all the work of your hands. When you knock down the fruit from your olive tree, do not go over the branches again. What remains will be for the resident alien, the fatherless, and the widow. When you gather the grapes of your vineyard, do not glean what is left. What remains will be for the resident alien, the fatherless, and the widow. Remember that you were a slave in the land of Egypt. Therefore I am commanding you to do this.

At the end of this passage, what specific reason did God give for treating the foreigner with kindness and generosity?

They were once slaves, aliens

PERSONAL REFLECTION: The Egyptians' racism toward the Hebrews was deplorable. According to the Deuteronomy passage, how did God use Israel's time in Egypt as a stark reminder of the need to treat outsiders among them differently?

Back to today's text in Genesis. What astonished the brothers, other than the fact that they were sitting at a lavish meal in the lord of Egypt's house? (Note the details of how they were seated.)

seated from eldest to youngest

Look back at Genesis 43:16. What was served at this meal? Given the famine, why was this so extraordinary? *meat*

I think of how the Israelites, years later, would grumble against God in the wilderness and ask, "Can God spread a table in the wilderness?" (Ps. 78:19b, ESV). The answer is, He'd already done it at Joseph's table in Egypt in the middle of a famine. And He'll spread His table again when He invites Christ's bride, His church, to sit down at the marriage feast of the Lamb (Rev. 19:9). This time not in the wilderness, but in heaven.

Then he said to me, "Write: Blessed are those invited to the marriage feast of the Lamb!" He also said to me, "These words of God are true."

Revelation 19:9

The food and wine at Joseph's table came from his personal allotment. We continue to see evidence of his forgiving and sacrificial attitude toward those who had hurt him, an attitude beyond most of our abilities to comprehend.

How was Benjamin's portion different than the other brothers'?

5x more

PERSONAL TAKE: What might be the reason Joseph had the brothers seated according to age and gave Benjamin extra portions? *acknowledgement*

It appears Joseph served extra portions to Benjamin to see if his brothers would react in anger and jealousy like they had done to him. At least at this point, it seemed they were passing the test.

I want you to make one more fascinating comparison. Look back at Genesis 37:23-25. What did the brothers sit down to do after throwing Joseph into the pit? How did this show the depth of their heartlessness?

No water or food

The tragic and horrific treatment of Joseph begins with a meal, and the beginnings of restoration between Joseph and his brothers end with a meal. Instead of the punishment the brothers deserve, they sit down to a lavish feast in the middle of a famine.

READ PSALM 103:8-14.

What does the psalmist reveal about God's nature toward us and how He deals with our sin? How do you see God's nature portrayed through Joseph's treatment of his brothers?

removes our sin
forgives their sin

Only God could have written this story. Only God could have fulfilled it.

God was piecing back together the hopelessly broken relationships of Jacob's twelve sons as they formed a peaceful union around the table. Only God could have written this story. Only God could have fulfilled it. Only God, in the midst of jealousy and hatred, could have brought *šalôm*.

DAY 5
THE SILVER CUP
GENESIS 44:1-17

Growing up in church I remember baptism Sundays being some of my favorite services of the year, and this wasn't just because we got out of a sermon. To this day, nothing inspires me more than Christ-followers talking about what Jesus has done in their hearts and lives. We're moved by these stories because they remind us that people like you and me, people who are broken and were once in despair, have been profoundly transformed by the person of Jesus. There's simply no other explanation for the dramatic renewal in our lives. I believe today's reading will serve as a reminder that when God is at work, people really can change.

When God is at work, people really can change.

READ GENESIS 44:1-17.

A quick note: The fact that Joseph's steward said the silver cup was used for divination was probably still part of Joseph's ploy to keep his identity hidden. Divination was later forbidden in Israel's culture, so it's unlikely Joseph used the cup for that purpose.[7]

> *Joseph put his brothers through a third and final test. In the space below, summarize this last test you just read about. I described the first two for you.*
>
> 1. *Joseph accused the brothers of being spies, imprisoned Simeon, and demanded the brothers bring Benjamin with them when they return for more grain (Gen. 42:9-20).*
>
> 2. *The brothers' silver was returned to their sacks, and it appeared they were thieves (Gen. 42:35).*
>
> 3. Places silver cup in Benj. sack. Accused of stealing. Keeping Benj. as slave

The brothers couldn't catch a break. Just when things seemed to be looking up they were accused of being spies, thrown in prison, framed with extra silver in their sacks, and now one of them appeared to have stolen Joseph's silver cup. Of course this was all by design.

PERSONAL TAKE: Based on what you've read so far, to what end do you think God was leading the brothers? Or to ask it another way, what do you believe this series of tests was designed to accomplish in the brothers' lives?

prof of their loyalty, honesty

In whose sack was the silver cup found and why was this significant? List every reason you can think of. Benj. –
to keep him close
to see if there was jealousy

How did the steward's prescribed punishment differ from what the brothers suggested their punishment should be (vv. 9-10)?
Benj slaves others blameless

> *"What can we say to my lord?" Judah replied. "How can we plead? How can we justify ourselves? God has exposed your servants' iniquity. We are now my lord's slaves—both we and the one in whose possession the cup was found."*
>
> Genesis 44:16

The wisdom of God was behind Joseph's masterful tests. Through each of the tests, God was working on the hearts of the brothers, while showing Joseph what kind of men his brothers had become. This last test was perhaps the most significant because it presented the brothers the opportunity to do to Benjamin what they had done to Joseph. "[Joseph] cannot trust himself to them until he knows that they are trustworthy."[8] Now that Benjamin had become the "guilty party," the rest of the brothers were free to abandon him and save themselves. If they still cared nothing about their father's heart and nothing about their half-brother Benjamin, they would sacrifice Benjamin as they sacrificed Joseph.

How did Judah respond on behalf of himself and his brothers (v. 16)?
I will take his place

LOOK BACK AT GENESIS 37:25-28.

Whose idea was it to sell Joseph? (Circle the best answer below.)
Reuben   Benjamin   Simeon   Judah

In what ways had Judah changed, and what brought about these changes?

PERSONAL TAKE: In Genesis 44:16, Judah says, "How can we plead? How can we justify ourselves? God has exposed your servants' iniquity." Since Judah knew he and the brothers weren't guilty of stealing the silver cup, what sin do you think Judah was talking about here?

selling Joseph

God was relentless. He wasn't going to stop chasing the brothers until they recognized what they'd done, faced their pasts, and ultimately acknowledged Him. While God's conviction may not feel good in the moment, the fact that He won't let us ignore our sin is, to me, one of His greatest characteristics. And while we may settle for being free of our guilt, God wants more for us: He removes it so we can freely enjoy our relationship with Him.

Have you ever been in a situation before the Lord where your thoughts were similar to Judah's: *How can I plead? How can I justify myself? God has exposed my sin.* Maybe you're in that situation right now. This conviction is the kindness of God's Holy Spirit stirring you, pleading with you to turn from your sin and receive forgiveness. Don't resist it; receive it by responding with repentance.

PERSONAL RESPONSE: If the Holy Spirit is convicting you of something, past or present, take a moment to write your confession before the Lord. If it requires sharing with another trusted person and/or making an apology, commit today to dealing with the sin.

Judah's confessional statement took place thousands of years before the cross of Christ and the unique indwelling of the Holy Spirit (not to mention before the Mosaic Law). Still, in Judah's response we sense God's conviction. Deep within our hearts we know our sin must be paid for and our guilt dealt with. Sometimes we try to make up for our sins by doing a bunch of good things in hopes of erasing the bad things, but the stains are still there. We try to numb our guilt through behaviors and activities that help us escape, but all these vain attempts just multiply our shame. Or, we try to build a worldview that either doesn't acknowledge sin or celebrates it, yet we're still left with the consequences. Humanity has tried to handle sin in countless ways, but only One has ever been able—and ever will be able—to forgive sin, to relieve guilt, and to wash away shame.

LOOK UP 1 JOHN 4:9-10.

In verse 9, how does John say God's love was revealed to us?

through Christ

According to verse 10, what is the ultimate definition of love?

God loves us and sent His Son as sacrifice for our sin

Your translation may say that Jesus was the atoning sacrifice for our sins or the propitiation. The Greek word is *hilasmos*, a very rich word about

*expiatory:
related to making
amends for or
extinguishing the
guilt incurred by
another party*[9]

which volumes have been written. *Vines Dictionary* says this about the word: "[Christ] Himself, through the expiatory sacrifice of His Death, is the Personal means by whom God shows mercy to the sinner who believes on Christ as the One thus provided."[10]

For our purposes, we can simply say that God is a holy God whose wrath must be poured out upon sin, otherwise He wouldn't be a God of justice. All sin must be paid for. Since we, as humans, are guilty sinners and unable to pay for our own sin, God sent His Son, Jesus Christ, to absorb God's wrath on our behalf. Jesus substituted His life for our lives. The apostle Paul in 2 Corinthians 5:21 says, "He made the one who did not know sin to be sin for us, so that in him we might become the righteousness of God."

If you've gone through this study without having pulled its thread of redemption straight into your own heart, will you do so now? Jesus is the Redeemer to whom this whole story points. Judah was willing to take the punishment for himself and his brothers, but Jesus blamelessly took our punishment for us on the cross, and that is just the beginning. Jesus invites us to follow Him through faith and repentance, learn from His teaching, and obey what He says. He gives us new hearts. This is not pie in the sky platitude or religious jargon. This is abundant life with Jesus.

PERSONAL RESPONSE: If you want to begin following Jesus, write a prayer of response below. In your own words, confess your sin, acknowledge that Jesus and Jesus alone has forgiven you because of His death and resurrection, and tell Him you want a relationship with Him. (See the appendix on p. 213.)

LET'S RETURN TO GENESIS 44:17.

PERSONAL TAKE: Judah pleaded for all the brothers to be taken as slaves, not just Benjamin. Why do you think Joseph insisted that only Benjamin be taken as a slave?

This is a precarious point in our story. If the brothers didn't pass the test of trying to save Benjamin it appeared all would be lost, for how would Joseph ever be able to trust them? But if they all became Joseph's slaves, what would happen to their father, Jacob, and their families left behind in Canaan, all of whom would starve in the famine? Only God could work this one out, just as He's worked out impossible situations like this since the beginning of time.

As we close today, let's contemplate the immense love God the Father has for us in sending His beloved Son, Jesus, to be our atonement. In the same vein as Judah we cry, *How can we justify ourselves when our sin is ever before us?* The truth is we can't. And that's precisely why Jesus has done it for us. What hymn says it better than this stanza from "It Is Well with My Soul"?

My sin—oh, the bliss of this glorious thought:

My sin—not in part, but the whole

Is nailed to the cross and I bear it no more,

Praise the Lord, praise the Lord, O my soul![11]

Contemplate the immense love God the Father has for us in sending His beloved Son, Jesus, to be our atonement.

SESSION 5 VIEWER GUIDE

EXTRAVAGANT MERCY

GROUP DISCUSSION

What portion of the video teaching really resonated with you? Why?

How did the video teaching about the mercy of God toward Jacob's family help you better understand the nature of Jesus' mercy toward us?

How does Joseph's gracious actions toward his brothers challenge you to show love to your own family members and loved ones—especially those who are the most difficult?

Maybe you've experienced guilt for an extended period of time. Since Jesus' love for you is infinitely greater than Joseph's love for his brothers, discuss practical steps you can take to live in the reality of His forgiveness.

Who in your life is God calling you to extend mercy to? Why might you be hesitant to do so?

The brothers initially resisted the idea of Joseph as their ruler. When have you resisted the Lord's prompting, only to later realize it was the Lord showing you mercy?

To access the video teaching sessions, use the instructions in the back of your Bible study book.

#FINDINGGODFAITHFUL

Apple Bundt Cake (serves 4–6)

INGREDIENTS

Apples:

1 cup chopped apple

2 tablespoons butter

1 tablespoon granulated sugar

2 tablespoons brown sugar

½ teaspoon cinnamon

Cake:

1 cup granulated sugar

1 cup brown sugar

½ cup butter

1 cup sour cream

½ teaspoon vanilla

5 large eggs

2½ cups flour

1 teaspoon baking soda

1 teaspoon baking powder

Pinch of salt

½ cup chopped walnuts

DIRECTIONS

Preheat the oven to 350 degrees. Butter a bundt cake pan, including the tube, and dust lightly with flour, shaking out any excess. Set aside.

In a skillet over medium heat, Cook the apples with the butter, sugars, and cinnamon. Don't overcook; apples should keep their shape. Set aside.

For the cake batter, combine sugars, butter, and sour cream in a large mixing bowl or stand mixer and beat until fluffy. Add vanilla and eggs until well combined. In a separate bowl, combine the flour, baking soda, baking powder, and salt.

Add the dry ingredients to the butter mixture. Fold in apples and walnuts. Bake at 350 degrees for about 40 minutes or until a toothpick inserted into the center of the cake comes out clean. Transfer cake to wire rack and let it cool in the pan for 10 minutes.

One of my favorite memories from growing up is going apple picking with my family at Stribling Orchard in Virginia. To this day I can get excited about any apple recipe, especially if it's made with autumn apples.

THE PROCESS OF FORGIVENESS

April 15th, better known as terrible Tax Day, has been reconstituted in my thinking as the day I can officially put my tomato plants in the ground without fearing frost. See what perspective does? I dig my trenches, lay the plants in a bit sideways, and cover them with soil before working in a measure of mushroom compost, manure, or worm castings. (Just when you thought you couldn't go lower than worms, they share their castings with us.) The year I started my tomato seeds indoors, all manner of heirloom varieties, it was hard to imagine how these diaphanous little flakes could transform into something as hearty and substantial as a tomato. But that year, I watched them run their race from seed to caprese salad. They sure showed me.

The funny thing about gardening is that you can hover over your plants, stare at them like you're trying to catch them in the act of growing, and never visibly perceive so much as a frame of change. They don't ever appear to be anything but paused. But give them a day or two, maybe a couple weeks, and vines will shoot off in unruly directions, yellow flowers will give way to green orbs, and weeds you didn't even know existed will positively take your vegetables hostage. Growth. Change. Life. It's the way the garden goes. But don't expect to witness a garden's progress in anything but stages. Garden plants won't give up all their secrets of growing and changing, only the whisper of evidence that they're doing so.

Gardening has taught me about seasons, patience, and persistence. I've learned that even when I can't visibly see it, growth is happening in my own life and in the lives of those around me. When I want to give up on daily obedience to Jesus for lack of visible progress, there lie the garden hoe of faithful study, the paring shears of cleansing prayer, and the well-worn gloves for serving others. "And let us not be weary in well doing," the Word says, "for in due season we shall reap, if we faint not" (Gal. 6:9, KJV).

I imagine Joseph to be weary at this point in the story. I imagine him wondering if any of his faithful interactions with his brothers have made a difference. The returned silver, the extra grain for their families, the lavish dinner at his table, his private tears—was it all for naught? Were transformation and reconciliation really possible? Would Egypt's grain be the only harvest Joseph would ever know, or was a crop of reconciled relationships on its way? Hint: When the Master Gardener is at work and we're laboring beside Him, the harvest may not come on our timetable, but it promises to be plentiful.

DAY 1
JUDAH AND TAMAR
GENESIS 38

Today we're going to hold our place in Genesis 44 and spend the day looking at a significant part of Judah's story in chapter 38. (You may remember, earlier in our study we skipped chapter 38 with the intention of returning to it.) As you've already noticed, Judah was emerging as the leader of the brothers and was taking his place as a significant character in our story. This would continue to be nothing short of shocking, especially since we already know that it was Judah's idea to sell Joseph into slavery. But that's just the half of it. Today we'll look at some other not-so-shiny moments in Judah's life, moments that took place after he sold his own brother into slavery.

God is weaving every detail together.

This section may feel like a break from Joseph's story, but as we continue to see how God is weaving every detail together, we'll begin to view this larger narrative not as Joseph's story or Judah's story, but as our Redeemer's.

READ GENESIS 38. THIS IS A LONGER PASSAGE THAN NORMAL, BUT GO AHEAD AND SETTLE IN FOR AN INTERESTING NARRATIVE. IT'S A CRAZY ONE FOR SURE, BUT NO ONE CAN SAY IT'S BORING.

I know what you're thinking. What in the world? How is this even in the Bible? You may have other questions like I do, some of which I hope we'll answer as we go. In the meantime, keep in mind that God can use any person and any circumstance to accomplish His promises. In some ways, I find that the crazier and more sordid Genesis 38 gets, the more faithful we find God to be. This may not all be clear today, but by the time we finish our study, I hope this truth will be remarkably evident.

Where in the time line of Joseph's story did Judah leave his homeland and marry a Canaanite woman? (See Gen. 37:36–38:1 for your answer.)

after brothers sold Joseph to Ismaelites

"The fact that the [Judah] narrative seems to lie outside the course of events of the Joseph story shows that the writer has put it here for a special purpose."[1] By inserting this chapter about Judah in the middle of the Joseph narrative, it seems the narrator wants us, as the reader, to juxtapose Judah's story with Joseph's story.

Draw a line to connect each statement to the brother it describes:

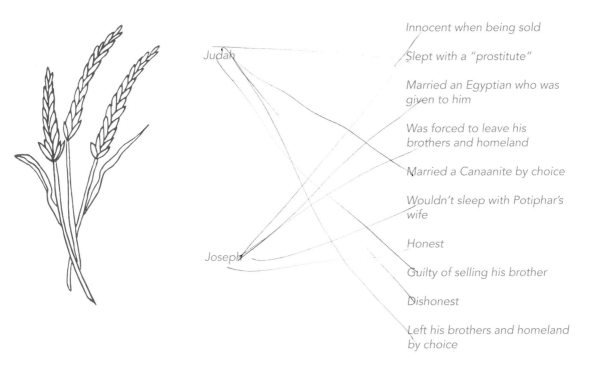

Judah

Joseph

Innocent when being sold

Slept with a "prostitute"

Married an Egyptian who was given to him

Was forced to leave his brothers and homeland

Married a Canaanite by choice

Wouldn't sleep with Potiphar's wife

Honest

Guilty of selling his brother

Dishonest

Left his brothers and homeland by choice

PERSONAL TAKE: For what purpose do you think the narrator wants us to compare and contrast Judah's and Joseph's stories?

According to Genesis 38:2, what nation was Judah's wife from?

Canaan

Look up Genesis 24:1-3 and 28:1-3. Abraham and Isaac did not want their sons to marry _____ women.
(Circle the best answer below.)

Loose   Widowed   Unattractive   Canaanite

The patriarchs forbade their sons from intermarrying with Canaanite women. This instruction wasn't motivated by racism or elitism. These unions were prohibited because the people living in the land of Canaan at the time were part of a pagan culture worshiping pagan gods. The Hebrews, on the other hand, were God's chosen people, set apart for His purposes and ultimately for the blessing of the entire world. By intermarrying with Canaanites who didn't worship or serve their God, the Hebrews' purpose as a nation would be compromised.

PERSONAL TAKE: After Judah sold Joseph into slavery, why do you think he left his brothers and married a Canaanite woman? Explain your answer.

guilt

You may have found it curious that each time Tamar's husband died before she was able to get pregnant the deceased husband's brother was expected to step in as her husband. This practice is called levirate marriage (Deut. 25:5-10), and it was about extending the family line (Gen. 38:8). If a man died without an heir, his brother was to marry the widow and produce a male heir. That son would then inherit the dead brother's name and property. The practice made sure the property remained within the family and the deceased brother's name would not be forgotten.[2] It also guarded against leaving a vulnerable widow without protection and provision.

> *Judah recognized them and said, "She is more in the right than I."*
>
> Genesis 38:26

Look back at verses 38:11,14. How did Judah deceive Tamar, and how would this have affected years of her life? *did not give her Shelah*

We can't underestimate the power that Judah held over Tamar. In withholding his third son from her, Judah relegated Tamar to her father's house, without a husband or the prospect of having a husband and without any hope to carry on her family line. Not to mention that Judah betrayed Tamar, having promised his son Shelah to her while never intending to follow through.

PERSONAL REFLECTION: How do you see this same abuse of power mixed with selfishness, deceit, and betrayal in our own culture? Think specifically. Although this story may initially seem far outside of our context, it's more relatable than we think.

When Judah found out that Tamar had disguised herself as a prostitute and she was the one he slept with, in what surprising way did he describe her (v. 26)? *acknowledged he had been deceptive - she more righteous*

I would have expected Judah to acknowledge his sin of sleeping with someone he thought was a prostitute, but what did he confess instead (v. 26)? she more righteous

PERSONAL REFLECTION: How do you think Judah's admission of his sin in this instance was important to his future transformation? very

When I confess my pride, jealousy, and selfishness—and I choose obedience—I'm encouraged to walk into further obedience.

I think it's significant that soon after Judah and his brothers sold Joseph into slavery Judah left his family and homeland. I think it's also significant that he ran straight into the arms of a Canaanite woman. Was he escaping his guilt? Had he hardened his heart and, as a result, chose to plunge further into selfishness and sin? I know firsthand my choice to sin can lead to more sin if I'm not repentant. But the opposite is also true. When I confess my pride, jealousy, and selfishness—and I choose obedience—I'm encouraged to walk into further obedience.

By leaving his Hebrew family and marrying a Canaanite woman, Judah demonstrated little regard for his role in the covenant family of God. Being part of what God was doing through His chosen people seemed of no importance to Judah. While we can't condone Tamar's methods, it seems she valued the significance of carrying on Judah's Hebrew family line. She could have fallen back into creating an empty legacy in Canaan, but instead she stayed loyal to Judah and his offspring. I believe this is why, despite her deceptive actions, Judah said that she acted more righteously than him.

The means don't justify the ends, but Tamar's radical commitment to follow God's law and carry on the precious line of Judah will secure her a renowned place in Israelite history. Scholar Bruce K. Waltke boldly asserts, "Normally Canaanite women absorb Israelite men into their debased culture (Deut. 7:1,3). In that light, [Tamar's] deception as a Canaanite prostitute to snare her widowed father-in-law into fathering covenant seed should be evaluated as a daring act of faith."[3]

LOOK BACK AT GENESIS 38:27-30.

Which of Judah and Tamar's twin sons was ultimately born first? (Circle the answer below.)

Perez   Zerah

At the risk of giving too much of the significance of our story away all at once, look up Matthew 1 and read verses 1-3. Judah's firstborn son is found in whose preeminent genealogy? David → Jesus

After writing today's study I met some friends for PG Tips and a splash of milk—they were visiting from England. They asked me if I'd had a good day and what I'd been writing about. Well now those are tricky questions when posed as a pair. Yes, I'd had a good day, but it's hard to follow that up with, *I wrote about Judah and Tamar and how Tamar lost her first two husbands because they were evil in the Lord's sight. Then Judah sent Tamar away and lied to her about his intention to give her his third son in marriage. So Tamar dressed up as a prostitute, and Judah slept with her. And then they had twin boys.* You can see my dilemma in answering their question. Can writing about all this really constitute having a good day?

I suppose the answer depends on one's perspective. Reading and writing about evil, betrayal, abuse of power, degradation of a woman's body, and heartbreak never makes for a good day. But our viewpoint broadens if we step back and consider this chapter through the lens of a few thousand years of hindsight. In those years we see God actively keeping His promises, fulfilling His covenant to Abraham, Isaac, and Jacob by bringing twin boys, one of whom would be in the line of Christ, out of a mess of a situation. God has been redeeming the undeserving and wounded like Judah, Tamar, you, and me, all along the way. If we can allow that truth to break through the darkness, then yes, today is a good day. A very good day, indeed.

DAY 2
A SUBSTITUTE
GENESIS 44:18-34

I'm so glad you're back after yesterday's tour through Genesis 38. That was no small feat. You can now see why there was simply no way we could ignore that detour in Judah's life, especially since he's taken center stage in Joseph's story. With all of Judah's history in mind—from his mother, Leah, praising the Lord at his birth, to his part in selling Joseph into slavery, to his rebellious journey from home, to betraying Tamar and sleeping with her, to his twin sons—we pick up with the next part of his story.

READ GENESIS 44:14-29. (LET'S START WITH A FEW VERSES FROM LAST WEEK SO WE CAN REMEMBER WHERE WE LEFT OFF.)

In three sentences or less, describe the essence of the dilemma that the brothers and their father, Jacob, were in.

without Benj. all die of starvation. with Benj. They all might be slaves

In the Christian Standard Bible (CSB), Genesis 44:16a reads, "'What can we say to my lord?' Judah replied. 'How can we plead? How can we justify ourselves? God has exposed your servants' iniquity.'" We looked at this verse on Day 5 of last week, but I want to revisit Judah's language in light of yesterday's study.

How was Judah's disposition in Genesis 44:16 similar to his disposition in Genesis 38:26? *Repentant*

Judah's rhetorical question in Genesis 44:16 is worded different ways in our English translations: "How can we justify ourselves?" "How can we prove our innocence?" "How can we clear ourselves?" One simple way to put it is, "How can we show ourselves to be right?"[4] This last rendition is helpful because it allows us to see that Genesis 38:26 and 44:16 share the same Greek root word *sadaq*. It means "to be in the right, be right; to be just."[5] (Remember from yesterday, Judah recognized his lack of righteousness as opposed to Tamar's.) In other words, this wasn't the first time Judah had pondered such things. And in his pondering he was coming up woefully short with absolutely no remedies.

Returning home from a trip to Moldova with JMI, I had my own Judah moment. After sitting with orphan girls who I may never see again, beholding a young girl whose eye had been punched out by a drunken stepfather, and meeting special needs children in impoverished environments, I found myself wondering if I had so much as a scrap of anything meaningful to offer anyone. The profound inadequacy I felt led to an awareness of my inability to save anyone and an awareness of my own sinfulness. Even if I had the power to make a sweeping difference in the country of Moldova, which I don't, I was still up against my selfishness, my pettiness, and my sin nature as a whole. I'm not quite sure how to explain it, but being among the poor and forgotten reminds me we are all laid bare before Jesus, on equal footing, all of us in need of a Savior. While I felt myself lamenting with Judah, *How can I clear myself?*, I reveled more deeply in the message of Romans 3:23-24: "For all have sinned and fall short of the glory of God. They are justified freely by his grace through the redemption that is in Christ Jesus."

For all have sinned and fall short of the glory of God. They are justified freely by his grace through the redemption that is in Christ Jesus.

Romans 3:23-24

PERSONAL REFLECTION: Can you think of a time when your sin was plainly before you and there was nothing you could do to justify it to God, others, or yourself? How did this deepen your appreciation for Jesus and His sacrifice for you?

As Judah recounted his story, he shared Jacob's words of lament about Joseph being torn to pieces (Gen. 44:28). Of course Judah couldn't say what really happened to his brother because that would have meant confessing to something immeasurably worse than one of them having stolen Joseph's silver cup. What a convoluted mess Judah and the brothers were in. Even in trying to tell the truth, Judah couldn't tell the whole truth because of his past offenses. And isn't that one of the worst feelings in the world?

PERSONAL RESPONSE: Perhaps, like Judah, you're trying to bring honesty to a current situation without having dealt with a past one. Is there something from your past that you still need to deal with, something that's getting in the way of your present? It can be as simple as writing a note to someone and asking for forgiveness or confessing a nagging fear to the Lord and having a friend remind you to trust Him. Take some time to process this question in the space below.

How do each of the following verses correlate with the place in which Judah and his brothers find themselves? Write a sentence next to each reference.
Proverbs 14:12

Romans 6:23

Galatians 6:7

God's grace is what shows us our sin in the first place and His grace is what rescues us from it.

While we can't truly ask for forgiveness without first grasping the weight and reality of our sin, God's love doesn't intend to leave us in our sin. As we've already discussed in our study, God's grace is what shows us our sin in the first place and His grace is what rescues us from it. John Newton said it best in "Amazing Grace," "'Twas grace that taught my heart to fear, and grace my fears relieved."[6] The tests that Joseph put his brothers through, as a result of God's leading, weren't for the sake of revenge but to lead them to repentance.[7]

PERSONAL TAKE: So far, how do we see Joseph's series of tests leading the brothers to repentance? Genesis 44:16 holds part of the answer.

admit their sin

Judah and his brothers were coming to grips with the horror of what they'd done to their brother Joseph and what they'd done to their father, Jacob, by bereaving him of his beloved son. Joseph's purpose in orchestrating this series of tests wasn't to condemn or destroy his brothers but to lead them to a place of restoration.

READ GENESIS 44:30-34.

How was Judah's attitude toward Benjamin different from his earlier attitude toward Joseph? Why was this significant?

He was willing to take Benj- place so as not to aggrieve his father

PERSONAL TAKE: Judah's deep concern for his father, Jacob, was obvious and compelling. Judah certainly didn't care about Jacob when he tried to kill Jacob's beloved son Joseph years earlier. What do you think brought about this change in Judah? *recognizing his powerlessness in the face of god*

What did Judah offer to do in verse 33 that proved his heart had significantly changed? *take Benj. place as slave*

Now please let your servant remain here as my lord's slave, in place of the boy. Let him go back with his brothers.

Genesis 44:33

I want you to hang on to Genesis 44:33 because it will be important near the end of our study. In the meantime, note that Judah was offering to be a substitute for Benjamin and the brothers. He was offering to stand in the place of their judgment. He was offering to take the penalty of Benjamin's "sin" of stealing the silver cup so everyone else could return home as free men, so their father, Jacob, wouldn't die of heartbreak, and so their families wouldn't die of starvation.

Slicing into this part of Joseph's story is like cutting into a layered cake. Not only was God working on a global level in carrying out His covenant with Abraham and his descendants, but God was also bringing about repentance in the hearts of Joseph's brothers and healing Joseph's wounds to bring together a fractured family. God is even using this story to work in our hearts all these years later. Only God can accomplish so many purposes with one story.

PERSONAL RESPONSE: My friend Emily had a great closing question for today's study. As you consider the greater story of redemption being woven together by the all-knowing God, how might He be accomplishing repentance and redemption in your own heart and story?

DAY 3
A STUNNING REVELATION
GENESIS 45:1-8

JOSEPH'S LIFE

● 17 years old:
Joseph sold into slavery

Today's reading needs no introduction, other than to say what you're about to read took place twenty-two years after Joseph last saw his father. Joseph was seventeen years old when God gave him dreams, followed by him being sold into slavery. Then there was a span of thirteen years—some of the time spent in Potiphar's house, some of it in a prison. Joseph was thirty years old when promoted to be Pharaoh's second-in-command, where he spent seven years overseeing the harvest. At the time of our reading, Joseph was two years into overseeing the seven years of famine.

READ GENESIS 45:1-8.

PERSONAL REFLECTION: What about this scene impacts you the most, and why? *length of time w/o family*

● 30 years old:
In the service of Pharaoh

● 39 years old:
Reveals himself to his brothers, two years into the famine

Out of all the moments Joseph could have chosen to reveal himself, why do you think he chose this moment? (Keep Judah's speech from Genesis 44:16-34 in mind.)

Far from wanting his brothers to endlessly suffer for what they'd done to him, all this time Joseph had been longing for them do the right thing. When Judah spoke on behalf of himself and his brothers and declared them all guilty before God, when he spoke tenderly about their father, Jacob, and finally, when he offered to be the one to suffer so everyone else could go free, that's when Joseph knew true repentance had taken place. "Judah's plea for Benjamin shows how sincerely they renounce their former sin (44:33–34)." [8]

PERSONAL TAKE: What are some specific characteristics of a truly repentant heart? List as many as you see in the life of Judah. Then list any other characteristics you can think of. *acknowledgement in front of others, action to make amends*

In this passage, Joseph wept again. What details reveal the extreme nature of his weeping? *Egyptians heard*

How many more years of famine were left (v. 6)? *5*

What was the first question Joseph asked his brothers after revealing his identity to them, and how did they respond? *Does my father still live*

Bros couldn't answer

There's no way for us to experience the same shock the brothers felt in that moment, partly because we've known all along that this harsh Egyptian lord was their innocent, suffering brother Joseph. His identity isn't new to us. But pause for a moment and consider the brothers' awe when the man who stood in charge of their fate, this Egyptian ruler, suddenly said to them with bloodshot eyes and a tear-drenched face, "I am Joseph!" (v. 3).

The brothers are described as being *dismayed, troubled,* or *terrified* at this news, depending on your translation. The definition of the Hebrew word *ba·hal* means to be " … alarmed, i.e., pertaining to being in a state of great fear, even causing trembling."[9]

PERSONAL TAKE: The answer to the following question may seem obvious, but do me the favor of thinking through your response. Why were the brothers absolutely terrified at Joseph's revelation? Give every reason you can think of. *worried @ revenge*

If we weren't aware of the work God had done in Joseph's heart, we would fully expect the brothers to be terrified in Joseph's presence because we'd fully expect Joseph to repay them for what they'd done. At the very least we would expect Joseph to execute justice.

What specific action did Joseph tell his brothers to take in verse 4? How was his tenderness different from everything we might have expected?

Come near to me

> *And now don't be grieved or angry with yourselves for selling me here, because God sent me ahead of you to preserve life.*
>
> Genesis 45:5

Thousands of years before the coming of Christ we're met here with a scene of forgiveness, reconciliation, love, grace, and affection that casts a gleaming light toward the good news of the gospel that will extend to every nation. Joseph was not treating his brothers as their sins deserved.

READ ROMANS 5:6-11.

How do these verses explain our state when Christ died for us? In other words, when Jesus gave His life for our salvation how deserving were we?

We were / are sinners

READ TITUS 3:3-7.

Paul lists specific sinful conditions we can all relate to. According to verses 4-5, what appeared to us in the middle of these conditions?

Holy Spirit

PERSONAL REFLECTION: Keeping in mind these verses from Romans and Titus, how is Joseph's overwhelming kindness toward his brothers a tangible picture of Christ's love for you? forgiveness, love, grace, redeem us

After Joseph revealed his identity initially, he revealed it a second time with a little extra detail. *I'm Joseph. You know, the brother you used to have, the one you sold into Egypt. Yeah, I'm that guy.* I've always found this humorous, as if Joseph was torturing them ever so slightly in a really nice, Joseph sort of way. But one commentator noted that Joseph was the only other person besides the brothers who would have known about what happened that terrible day in Dothan. Giving this extra detail was Joseph's way of proving his identity to his brothers.[10]

What did Joseph surprisingly tell his brothers not to be in Genesis 45:5? Does this bother you? Encourage you? Explain your reaction.

don't be grieved or angry with yourself

What reasons did Joseph give for telling his brothers not to be grieved or angry with themselves? (See vv. 5-8.)

God has a plan for us to save our family

PERSONAL REFLECTION: How does embracing God's perspective of a situation help us reframe even the worst things that have happened to us?

PERSONAL REFLECTION: When life is so dark that you can't see God's perspective or His purpose, how does His presence with you encourage and comfort you? (Think of the many times the author of Genesis told us God was with Joseph, even in the hardest times.)

Look back at Genesis 45:8. Who did Joseph say sent him to Egypt? (Circle your answer below.)

Judah   Simeon   Reuben   God

PERSONAL TAKE: Three times in the course of verses 5-8, Joseph stated it was God who had sent him to Egypt. How do you reconcile this statement with the fact that his brothers had sold him into slavery? *God allowed it to happen — turned sin to blessing*

> God is able to work out His divine purposes in your life, not only in spite of the pain others have caused you but also because of that pain.

Verse 8 is one of a few darts in Scripture that lands straight in the bull's-eye of God's mysterious sovereignty. We'll deal with this idea further when we reach chapter 50. I hope you'll find comfort in knowing that God is able to work out His divine purposes in your life, not only in spite of the pain others have caused you but also because of that pain. He is able to take whatever good, bad, or indifferent actions people have taken toward you and not merely salvage them, but somehow, in ways we can't understand, orchestrate them for His purposes and your good.

This might be terrifying news if we didn't know, from other parts of the Bible, that God is altogether good, there is no darkness in Him, and He is incapable of evil (Num. 23:19; Ps. 145:9; 1 John 1:5). I can't say I completely grasp how all this fits together. But we'll find out later in our story that God didn't pretend the sin of what the brothers did to Joseph didn't exist or wasn't a big deal. God is a God of justice, and He takes seriously the sin others inflict on us. He's not sweeping their terrible actions under the rug—we'll spend more time on this in the last week of our study. In the meantime, I want to focus on God's sovereignty over Joseph's life and how even the evil actions of his brothers could never keep God from accomplishing His purposes.

Who would specifically benefit as a result of Joseph being sent ahead of his family to Egypt? (See v. 7.) Brothers

This grace we received from Christ came while we were still sinners. A grace we didn't deserve.

I recently heard an old hymn for the first time. This hymn describes Jesus' return and how when He comes back a whole bunch of people are going to meet their doom. It is set to a peppy tune, so that was a little disconcerting. I'm not skirting the reality of God's coming judgment. But the part of Jesus' return that deserves the lively melody is His saving of us from such doom. We will dwell in His presence forever and ever, amen. Someone set that to some music!

The day after I'd heard that hymn, my friend Angela asked me where I was in Joseph's story. I told her I was writing about the scene where Joseph revealed himself to his brothers. She shot back with, "Are you gonna write about how Joseph didn't start singing the song about how all of the brothers were about to meet their doom?" And you know what? I am going to write about that. Because Angela's right—that's not the song Joseph sang. He sang a song of forgiveness, mercy, goodness, and kindness. If we could name that song I think it would be called "Grace."

Is anyone else as moved as I am in this moment by the grace of God flowing through Joseph toward his brothers? Joseph had once worn a robe of many colors, now he wore a robe of many Christlike qualities. The first was torn and dipped in blood. The latter would only come about in full because of Christ's torn body and shed blood for us. This grace we received from Christ came while we were still sinners. A grace we didn't deserve. A grace that met us as a result of Jesus' suffering, not our own. This gospel grace that rescued us was foreshadowed by the "great deliverance" Joseph described in his day (v. 7). Now we've experienced an infinitely greater deliverance since Jesus was raised from the dead, having redeemed us from our sin.

As God used sinful men like Joseph's brothers to bring about a great deliverance for the Israelites and the whole world, so God used sinful men to put Jesus to death to bring about deliverance for all who would trust and follow Him. Acts 2:23-24 says, "Though he was delivered up according to God's determined plan and foreknowledge, you used lawless people to nail him to a cross and kill him. God raised him up, ending the pains of death, because it was not possible for him to be held by death."

The brothers must have expected Joseph's fury and wrath to be unleashed on them at his revelation. Instead Joseph said those four glorious words, "Please, come near me" (v. 4).

CLOSE TODAY'S STUDY BY READING HEBREWS 10:19-23.

The author of Hebrews tells us that we can _____ in full assurance. (Circle the best answer below.)

Stand back   Fearfully Approach   Tearfully Approach   Draw Near

I hope today's section of Joseph's story has awakened a new affection in you for God, His Son, Jesus, and the salvation He's brought us. A judgment is coming, but we need not fear it if we've been cleansed once and for all by the blood of Jesus shed for us on the cross.

PERSONAL RESPONSE: As Joseph asked his undeserving brothers to come near to him, how have you heard God's call to draw near to Him today? Respond to Him. He's singing that song called "Grace."

DAY 4
A STUNNING REDEMPTION

GENESIS 45:9-24

I grew up in an environment where often the message was, Do the right thing, and you'll be blessed. Don't do the right thing, and you'll be punished. As a stand-alone concept, this has a measure of truth to it, but it doesn't take grace into account. It doesn't allow for God's love expressed through the person of Jesus to step in and give us what we don't deserve and spare us from what we do deserve. Certainly we believe in this grace as it relates to our salvation. But do we miss this grace in our everyday lives, mistakenly thinking that God is not in the business of being lavishly good to us, especially when we haven't earned it or blatantly don't deserve it?

Do we miss this grace in our everyday lives, mistakenly thinking that God is not in the business of being lavishly good to us, especially when we haven't earned it or blatantly don't deserve it?

Today we're going to read about the tangible, everyday grace that showed up with its boots on the ground for an undeserving group of people, Jacob and his sons. There's just no other way to describe the grace we're going to read about other than calling it amazing.

SLOWLY TAKE IN GENESIS 45:9-15 TODAY.

PERSONAL TAKE: What part of Joseph's gracious offer moves you the most, and why? *He wants his family to be near*

Who continued to be Joseph's focus throughout the famine (vv. 9,13)? *his father*

Joseph wanted his father, Jacob, to know that God had made him "lord of all Egypt" (v. 9). Joseph could have touted his own perseverance, scrappiness, and mental toughness in reaching this powerful position. He could have attributed it to fate, good vibes, or the cooperation of the universe. Instead, he gave glory to God as the only One who could have achieved and pieced his success together.

PERSONAL REFLECTION: When we think back on the hard, even impossible, times in our lives that God has redeemed, sometimes we put the focus on our own strength and intellect. In what ways can you specifically give God the glory for the redemption He's brought about in your life?

What part of Egypt did Joseph tell his family they could settle in? (Circle the best answer below.)

(Goshen)   Dothan   Canaan   Cairo

List everyone and everything Joseph told his brothers to bring back to Egypt with them (v. 10): flocks, families, Jacob

Sometimes we forget that our obedience not only affects us but the people around us, even those we might not know. Joseph's surrender and obedience to the Lord throughout these twenty-two years was now working out an incomprehensible salvation for generations of people he'd never even met—in the middle of a devastating famine. Obedience to Christ may not come easy but the blessings are without rival.

PERSONAL REFLECTION: How does the impact Joseph had on countless lives—from newborn babies all the way up to those the age of his father—inspire you to follow Christ no matter the cost? God has one track, a plan for us - plans to prosper us, not harm us

To me, part of what is so compelling and touching about today's Genesis reading is the personal nature of Joseph's disposition toward his brothers. "Joseph gives up his power of knowledge, whereby he controlled his brothers, for the embrace of intimacy with them."[11] Joseph now invited his family to come live near him (v. 10). He told them he would sustain them (v. 11). Up to this point Joseph protected himself by keeping his brothers at a distance through his knowledge and power over them. But when the right time came, he relinquished these protective measures out of love and care for his family. Joseph's promise in verse 11 uses the word _sustain,_ a word used in other parts of Scripture to describe God's care for us.

LOOK UP PSALM 55:22.

What does the psalmist tell us to do so we can experience the sustaining provision of the Lord? cast our burdens on the Lord

CONTINUE BY READING GENESIS 45:16-24. AS YOU READ, MENTALLY NOTE JOSEPH AND PHARAOH'S DETAILED CARE OF THE BROTHERS, THEIR FAMILIES, AND LIVESTOCK.

PERSONAL TAKE: After reading about the specific care Joseph and Pharaoh gave the brothers in this section, what one word comes to mind? Write it in all caps below. (There's no right answer, just write whatever word you think best describes their gifts and actions.) *GRACE, ABUNDANCE*

Your Word:

I would love to know the word you came up with. Whatever it is, it's probably an attribute of our God because God is the One behind this great deliverance. The word that immediately came to my mind after reading this section is *lavish*. Pharaoh and Joseph lavishly cared for them—from the invitation for every family member to come to Egypt, to a pastureland for their herds and flocks, to provision from the best of all the land of Egypt during a famine, to enormous wagons that would serve as moving trucks, to changes of clothing, extra silver, gift baskets for Jacob, grain for the journey—all for the undeserving. I'm utterly astounded and not merely at Joseph and Pharaoh's kindness—though it is impressive—but at God's goodness toward Joseph's family. The story just can't be any clearer—this colossal rescue was no one's idea but God's, not to mention His doing.

> *Look back at Jacob's statement just before he sent all his sons to Egypt in Genesis 43:14. How has God exceedingly and abundantly answered Jacob's hope that God would move "the man" to show mercy?*
>
> *Abundantly*

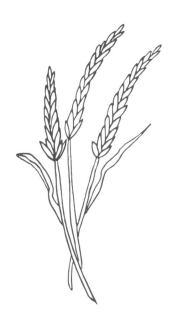

God's lavish abundance is on display in several areas, but I want to draw our attention to one verse in particular: Genesis 45:18. Here Pharaoh offered Joseph's family the "fat/richness of the land," and this unique expression was used only here in the Bible.[12] In the middle of scarcity, God was able to provide Jacob's family with the finest the land had to offer.

> *What did Pharaoh tell Joseph's family not to be concerned about in verse 20?* *Your goods*

Even though Pharaoh was sending the provision of wagons (moving trucks) with the brothers, the wagons were for the people (v. 19). There was no need to shove the ancient Near Eastern equivalent of grandma's antique chest, their brand new fifty-two-inch television, or a favorite recliner into the truck. Pharaoh encouraged traveling light and leaving some things behind for the abundance of what was ahead. (We'll see tomorrow in Gen. 46:6 that they may not have listened and took their possessions, but the principle remains.)

Why did Pharaoh tell them not to worry about bringing all their stuff (v. 20)?

He would provide the best

I can't help but think of the parable Jesus told in Luke 15 about a father and his two sons. The younger son asked his father for an early portion of his inheritance, ran off, and squandered the money. After a time of suffering, the wayward prodigal came to his senses and returned home. The father greeted him with feasting and a celebration. The older brother who had seemingly remained faithful to his father, yet had never had a party like this was infuriated by this turn of events. The father replied, "Son … you are always with me, and everything I have is yours" (Luke 15:31).

Just as Pharaoh told Joseph's brothers not to lament anything they would have to leave behind because the best of the land would be theirs, so Jesus reminds His followers that no matter what we're experiencing, God's abundance is ours in Christ (2 Cor. 1:20; 1 Tim. 6:17; 2 Pet. 1:3). If you're like me, you tend to lament the stuff you can't fit into the wagon—the stuff you've had to leave behind in the course of following Jesus. But what is any of that when the best of all the land, the abundant life in Christ, awaits you?

PERSONAL RESPONSE: Is there anything you're clinging to, anything you don't want to let go of, because you don't trust the provision God has for you? Take some time to offer whatever it is—relationship, job, possession—to God. Everything He has is yours. And, better yet, He is always with you.

His divine power has given us everything required for life and godliness through the knowledge of him who called us by his own glory and goodness.

2 Peter 1:3

I believe one of the primary reasons Joseph was able to forgive and show love to his brothers was because He had experienced God's provision and presence in his life. Joseph knew his experience in Egypt wasn't some cosmic accident or the triumph of his brothers' evil. He clearly recognized God's hand in his life, and perhaps he recognized God's work in the grander narrative of keeping His covenant with Abraham and his descendants. Joseph was able to love his brothers because he knew and experienced God's love for himself.

First John 4:10-11 says, "Love consists in this: not that we loved God, but that he loved us and sent his Son to be the atoning sacrifice for our

We can only truly love others out of the overflow of God the Father and Jesus' love for us.

sins. Dear friends, if God loved us in this way, we also must love one another."

PERSONAL RESPONSE: We can only truly love others out of the overflow of God the Father and Jesus' love for us. What's one specific way you can show love to someone in response to Christ's love for you? Describe it below and commit to following through.

A GREAT SALVATION

GENESIS 45:25–46:27

You may have heard the expression in sports or in politics that one side is playing checkers while the other is playing chess. I wasn't very good at either of those games—I've always needed a ball in my hands—but what I do know is that checkers involves a lot of quick, reactive moves while chess is more complex and requires strategic forethought. It's playing the short game versus the long game.

I am queen of the short game in case you were wondering. On my bad days, I measure God's favor toward me (or lack thereof) by whatever has gone right or wrong that day. When I do this, I forget that not only is God after the long game in my life—my personal sanctification, spiritual growth, blessing of others, heart growing to look more like Christ's—He's also after His long game. In other words, God cares deeply about our individual lives, and at the same time, He wants to use us in His far bigger story of redemption. We're meant for something much larger than ourselves, but this is easy to forget in our instant gratification and selfie culture.

I bring all this up because we've recently been looking on as Jacob's family members have each made a lot of individual checker moves. But today we're about to be astounded and comforted by the long plan God has had from the beginning and is still fulfilling to this day. And, sidenote, it's a plan we get to be part of.

God cares deeply about our individual lives, and at the same time, He wants to use us in His far bigger story of redemption.

READ GENESIS 45:25-28.

PERSONAL REFLECTION: The brothers could have first told Jacob about their encounter with Pharaoh, their new clothes, the extra provisions, Benjamin's silver and the banquet they had in Egypt. Instead they led with "Joseph is still alive!" (v. 26). What does this say about how their values had changed?

Describe Jacob's two contrasting responses upon hearing the news that Joseph was still alive. heart stood still. spirit revived

What specifically did Jacob see that convinced him Joseph was still alive (v. 27)? (Circle the best answer below.)

An angel   Donkeys   Benjamin   ~~Wagons~~

PERSONAL TAKE: Out of all the things Jacob could have seen that would have convinced him Joseph was alive, why do you think it was the wagons that did it?

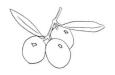

But God proves his own love for us in that while we were still sinners, Christ died for us.

Romans 5:8

PERSONAL REFLECTION: Have you ever experienced the revival of a dream you thought had died? How did this experience draw you closer to the Lord or show you something about His power and love?

It's important to note Jacob's numbed heart and lack of belief (v. 26) contrasted with his revived heart and belief. We see in other parts of the first five books of the Old Testament (The Pentateuch) how much God values faith and belief in Him. Revived hearts can believe; numb hearts cannot. This is why we take comfort in the prophets foretelling about a Savior who would one day come to give us new hearts and a new spirit (Jer. 31:31-33; Ezek. 36:26), so we, too, could believe.

I've always loved the picture of the gray-haired, aged, and emotionally-wounded Jacob lifting his head back to life, revitalized at what could have only seemed like a miracle to him—receiving his son back from the dead as it were. And I equally love that what helped Jacob turn the corner from unbelief to belief was the appearance of those Egyptian wagons. "Perhaps the grain, animals, and gifts could have been bought with the silver [the brothers] had in hand or had stolen, but not the wagons."[13]

Just like Jacob's faith wasn't blind, neither is ours. God through Christ has shown us Himself, and He's shown us His love through Jesus' death on the cross. I can't help but think of Romans 5:8, "But God *proves* his own love for us in that while we were still sinners, Christ died for us" (*emphasis mine*).

PERSONAL REFLECTION: What "wagons" has God brought you that have softened your heart and revived your faith in Him?   *Western Wall*

CONTINUE BY READING GENESIS 46:1-7.

Jacob had seen enough to convince him Joseph was still alive, and so he set out with all his family for Egypt.

What was the name of the first place Jacob stopped?

Beersheba

What did Jacob do there? *offered sacrifices*

Beer-sheba is a significant place in the overall story of Genesis. Let's look at some other important events that happened there.

What took place in Beer-sheba according to the following verses? Put a short description next to each passage:
Genesis 21:33 (Abraham's experience) *covenant before enemies*

Genesis 26:23-24 (Isaac's experience) *God appeared to Isaac saying God will bless and multiply descendents*

Both Abraham and Isaac experienced important moments with God in Beer-sheba. Now it was Jacob's turn to call upon the God of his fathers in the same place they had.

After Jacob offered sacrifices to the Lord, the Lord spoke to him that night in a vision. What did God tell Jacob not to be afraid of (Gen. 46:3-4)? *going to Egypt*

Look back at Genesis 26:2-3. How were God's instructions to Isaac different than what he told Jacob in Genesis 46? *Told Isaac not to go to Egypt*

God had specifically told Jacob's father, Isaac, not to go to Egypt, and He'd specifically led Jacob to the promised land of Canaan. Jacob might have been concerned about leaving Canaan for Egypt. He may have wondered if Joseph's and now all of his family's descent into Egypt ran counter to God's plan for his family and the generations to come. This move represented not only an enormous shift in location but also a shift in thinking. This doesn't mean God is fickle or unreliable, rather He was following His specific plan of redemption that was much larger than anyone could have possibly understood at the time.

PERSONAL REFLECTION: Have God's actions ever seemed to run counter to something you thought was His will? (Keep in mind, He'll never run counter to His Word or His Holy Spirit.) What did this situation teach you about Him?

According to Genesis 46:3, what did God say He would accomplish in Egypt? He would make Jacob a great nation there

TRUE/FALSE: *God promised great things for Jacob in Egypt, but Jacob and his family would have to go without God's presence since they were heading into a pagan land.*

PERSONAL REFLECTION: What encouragement do you receive from knowing that God's presence would accompany Jacob even to a place as godless and foreign as Egypt?

Genesis 46:5 says, "Jacob left Beer-sheba. The sons of Israel took their father Jacob in the wagons Pharaoh had sent to carry him … " This imagery shows that Jacob was too weak to leave his home and lead his family to Egypt.[14] His sons would have to shoulder the responsibility to transport him there. Waltke points out, "The promises will not be realized through human strength but through divine grace. His sons now take charge in carrying out the migration."[15]

This was a great reminder for me. So often I weary myself, running here and there with my hair on fire, wheels spinning, toiling and striving to accomplish God's plan for Him, trying to make up for my failures, when—breaking news—I'm ultimately not capable and He's already accomplished it. Our human strength is not what's going to do the trick, only His divine grace will do.

PERSONAL RESPONSE: How does this image of Jacob's sons putting their father in none other than the Egyptian Pharaoh's wagons show you God has you and your life in His hands, fully able to accomplish His purposes in and through you?

Our human strength is not what's going to do the trick, only His divine grace will do.

Look again at verse 7. Who came with Jacob to Egypt? all the descendants

We're given an important note in verses 5–7. This rescue wasn't for a chosen few. All of the brothers' dependents, their wives, and children came along too. We don't get all the details, "[n]evertheless, they too— even those from a Canaanite wife and an Egyptian wife—are known by name and numbered among God's people."[16] Because Jacob's descendants are so important to God's overall story of redemption, the author of Genesis includes the specific names of the sons born to Leah and her maidservant and Rachel and her maidservant and even lists the son's sons (Jacob's grandchildren) by name.

FINISH TODAY'S STUDY BY READING GENESIS 46:8-27.

Before you think about skipping this genealogy, please allow me to guilt you into reading each name. It's valuable for several reasons. First, you may see some interesting things based on previous knowledge—recognizing some names of people you've learned about in our study so far. Plus, it's a good exercise to familiarize yourself with the names of the leaders that will form the twelve tribes of Israel. And the list is a good reminder that God uses real people with actual names, like you and me, to accomplish His purposes.

So far in our study we've been mostly looking at Joseph's story from a checkerboard perspective—lots of reactionary and sometimes unrelated moves that don't seem to be governed by a bigger plan. We're finally at a point where we're beginning to see God's much bigger plan of redemption playing out, a plan marked by patience and forethought. We're beginning to see that God, in and through all the little moves of His people in our story—some sacrificial, some selfish—is working out a great plan to turn the house of Jacob into the nation of Israel in the land of Egypt.[17]

One might say all the players in Joseph's story were playing checkers while God was playing chess. Except God isn't playing a game with kings, queens, pawns, and knights. He's writing a story of redemption that's all about one King whose name is Jesus—the King who will rescue His people from their sins.

He's writing a story of redemption that's all about one King whose name is Jesus—the King who will rescue His people from their sins.

SESSION 6 VIEWER GUIDE

THE PROCESS OF FORGIVENESS

GROUP DISCUSSION

What portion of the video teaching really resonated with you? Why?

Why is forgiveness difficult for us? How does the difficulty of forgiving someone who wronged you require the help and power of Jesus?

Share a time someone extended overwhelming forgiveness to you. What effect did it have on your heart?

Which of these words better describes the way you use your authority: condemning or rescuing? Explain. How can you be more gracious?

Joseph knew it was God who had sent him to Egypt despite his brothers selling him there. How does God's Word help you gain His perspective on the difficult situations in your life?

Is there currently someone you need to forgive or seek forgiveness from? What's holding you back?

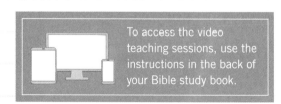

To access the video teaching sessions, use the instructions in the back of your Bible study book.

#FINDINGGODFAITHFUL

Double-Hot Oven Fried Chicken (serves 10–12)

INGREDIENTS

1½ cups buttermilk

2 tablespoons olive oil

2 tablespoons hot pepper sauce

2 tablespoons dijon mustard

2 cloves garlic, minced

Salt and black pepper, to taste

1 large onion, chopped

12 pieces of chicken

    (legs, thighs, and breasts)

2 cups unseasoned bread crumbs

⅓ cup Parmesan cheese

¼ cup flour

1 teaspoon ground thyme

1 teaspoon ground paprika

Cayenne pepper, to taste

Garnish: ¼ cup chopped

    chives

DIRECTIONS

In a large bowl, mix together buttermilk, olive oil, hot pepper sauce, dijon mustard, garlic, salt, pepper, and onion. Add chicken pieces, coating well. Cover bowl with plastic wrap and refrigerate at least 3 hours, turning chicken occasionally.

Preheat your oven to 350 degrees. In another bowl, combine bread crumbs, Parmesan cheese, flour, thyme, paprika, and cayenne pepper (if using). Individually dredge pieces of chicken in breadcrumb mixture and place on a rimmed baking sheet in a single layer. Bake at 350 degrees for about 50 minutes or until golden brown and an instant-read thermometer inserted at the thickest part of the chicken reads 165 degrees. Top chicken with chives.

Hot chicken has been a staple in my hometown of Nashville for many years. I thought it would be fun to include a recipe in honor of this tradition, one that can feed a large group or large family. It's perfect for get-togethers, and who couldn't use another spin on chicken?

A REDEMPTION STORY

Writing my first cookbook, *A Place at the Table*, was unlike any process I'd ever experienced. First of all, you don't really write a cookbook as much as you cook one and then eat your way through it. When my dear friend Regina Pinto, who also happens to be a renowned chef, and I decided to embark on this culinary adventure together, we had no idea what we were in for. Besides the painstaking task of gathering and testing recipes, grouping them in a meaningful fashion, and writing stories about them, we had to photograph all these creations.

More goes into cookbook photography than I could have possibly imagined. The first day of our shoot, Regina and I nervously pulled up to a building that was half test kitchen and half studio. Regina's responsibility was to swiftly prep and cook more than one hundred recipes in approximately nine days—I have no idea what she was so worried about. When they were ready for the camera, Teresa, our extraordinary food stylist, dressed each dish with finishing touches, such as chopped herbs, shaved chocolate, or perfectly piped icing depending on the recipe. A single stem bouquet here, a brass ladle there, a perfectly strewn napkin for good measure, and our photographer,

Stephanie, was ready to snap the picture. If you're wondering what I did all those days, I was very busy "testing."

I'm indebted to this talented team because photography is essential to a cookbook. You have to visually portray what you're hoping your readers will cook. You can't just tell them; you have to show them. I found myself gazing at certain creations and thinking, *So that's what berry panna cotta looks like*, or *I've never been confident preparing a charcuterie board, but now I can see it!* Pictures often tell us what words can't. Ironically, the opposite is also true: A cookbook full of beautiful pictures without any recipes would be a recipe for disaster. The success of your meal is dependent on a list of ingredients, exact measurements, and step-by-step directions. We need both image and instruction.

What I've always found particularly meaningful about the Bible is that it's both of these. In some instances the Bible gives us specific direction, while other portions are filled with exciting and compelling stories to show us more than they tell us. As we enter into our second to last week of *Finding God Faithful*, I encourage you to consider what you've observed about God and His attributes. Note what you've discovered about human behavior and how our choices to obey or disobey God affect our relationships with Him and one another. In many ways Joseph's story shows more than it instructs. But if writing a cookbook has taught me anything, it's a good picture can tell us as much as a good recipe.

DAY 1
AN UNTHINKABLE REUNION

GENESIS 46:28-30

I wonder in what ways the Lord has done the impossible and the utterly amazing in your life. This could be anything from the joy of your salvation to bearing a child the doctors were certain you couldn't have. Perhaps it was meeting the love of your life after a devastating divorce or years of singleness. Or bankruptcy turned profitable business. Or maybe it was being cured from something no one thought curable, or the restoration of a relationship that was as good as dead. God is in the business of performing the impossible. Yes, for our future salvation through His death and resurrection, but also in the here and now—in the land of the living—through His life (Ps. 27:13; Rom. 5:10). We're going to get a picture of God's impossible work in today's study. Praise Him. My soul needs it.

Today's reading opens the final scene of our story. We'll spend the next two weeks reflecting on the wealth of events that happens during these chapters but know we're transitioning into the final act of our story (sniff, sniff).

God is in the business of performing the impossible.

READ GENESIS 46:28-30.

PERSONAL REFLECTION: What grips you the most about Joseph and Jacob's reunion and why? Describe. *fell and wept on his neck*

Who did Jacob send ahead of the family to notify Joseph of his arrival in Goshen? (Circle your answer below.)

(Judah)   Reuben   Asher   Benjamin

Look back at Genesis 37:26-28. Why is this choice unexpected?
He was the one who sold him

(Don't forget that Judah's place in this story continues to grow in significance. Hang on to these mentions of him as they'll culminate in a dramatic way in the final week of our study.)

More than twenty years ago, Judah split up father and son when he sold Joseph into slavery. Now we see him preparing the way for Joseph and Jacob's reunion. I have to believe the irony wasn't lost on Judah as he left his family and made the lonely trek to Egypt. Along that journey Judah surely recognized how God orchestrated all that happened, not to mention God's kindness to someone as undeserving as him—Judah's life was being spared during the worst of famines by the brother he'd sold into slavery. Certainly he would have recognized both the sovereignty and mercy of God.

> *What did Joseph do when he heard his father Jacob was in the land of Goshen (v. 29)? What kind of picture does this paint about Joseph's expectation?*
>
> *Made ready to meet him*

It appears Joseph tore out of Egypt with urgency, dust swirling in his wake, soaring through the plains to see his father. After more than twenty years of suffering, prosperity, and waiting—a lot of waiting—it was time to be reunited with his beloved father.

> *Return to the Personal Take on Day 2 of Session 4 (p. 76) and look at the meaning of Manasseh's name. Whose house had Joseph "forgotten"?*
>
> *his family's*

Joseph hitched the horses to his chariot and went up to Goshen to meet his father Israel. Joseph presented himself to him, threw his arms around him, and wept for a long time.

Genesis 46:29

PERSONAL REFLECTION: What does Jacob and Joseph's reunion tell you about God's faithfulness, even when we've given up hope?

Describing their reunion, the CSB translation says, "Joseph presented himself to him, threw his arms around him, and wept for a long time" (Gen. 46:29b). Your version may say Joseph "appeared" to Jacob. The Hebrew word for *appeared* (*presented*), *wayyera*, is used to describe God's appearing to Abraham, Isaac, and Jacob in earlier parts of Genesis. It's also used later in the account of the burning bush appearing to Moses (Ex. 3:2). While Joseph's appearing to Jacob wasn't a theophany (God appearing to a human) like the other examples of the use of *wayyera* we've referenced, the author of Genesis wants us to see that God was in Jacob and Joseph's reunion.[1] This moment of reconciliation wasn't a result of happenstance or even an occasion God merely allowed to happen—He was in this.

PERSONAL REFLECTION: Think of a time when you definitively experienced the Lord in your life. Have you thought about it recently? Have you thanked Him for it? Briefly write what you learned about God and His presence through that experience. *He is real*

After Joseph and Jacob's emotional reunion, Jacob said, "I'm ready to die now because I have seen your face and you are still alive!" (Gen. 46:30). This isn't the first time in Jacob's life when seeing someone's face was a divine experience. Earlier in his life, Jacob cheated his older brother, Esau, out of his birthright and deceived their father into giving Jacob the family blessing, even though it was supposed to go to the oldest son, Esau. Animosity boiled over to the point that Jacob fled his homeland because Esau vowed to murder him. Many years later the two brothers were set to meet again.

READ GENESIS 33:1-10.

How did Jacob describe seeing his brother, Esau, after being terrified to see him (v. 10)? *like seeing the face of God*

PERSONAL TAKE: Why do you think Jacob described this event in this way?
relieved, thankful

Though Jacob experienced remarkable encounters with God, the truth is, we have greater access to "God's face" than any of the people we've been studying in Genesis. I love reading about these exceptional moments in history because they remind me that any glimpses of God in the Old Testament are meant to point us to what we have in our glorious and divine Savior, Jesus Christ.

READ 2 CORINTHIANS 4:4-6.

How is the light of the knowledge of God's glory displayed to us?
in the face of Jesus

READ COLOSSIANS 1:15,19-20.

How has God shown Himself to us?

As a daughter of Christ, who dwells within you?

Christ

Today, we have all the fullness of Christ in us through the presence of the Holy Spirit, not to mention the blessing we have in His Word and His church. Let's lean into these realities for the remarkable blessings they are.

In Jacob's day, the divine and dramatic experiences of God's presence kept God's people going for years at a time, sometimes decades. They didn't have the indwelling of the Holy Spirit, the fellowship of the body of Christ, or access to God through the person of Jesus the way we do now (Heb. 4:16; 10:19-22). Every now and again someone would have an extraordinary experience with God that would redirect the steps of God's people or turn them back to Himself. Today, we have all the fullness of Christ in us through the presence of the Holy Spirit, not to mention the blessing we have in His Word and His church. Let's lean into these realities for the remarkable blessings they are.

PERSONAL RESPONSE: What can you bring to the Lord right now as a result of having access to the Father through Jesus Christ? What is burdening you? Is there something you're longing for? Share it with Him because your Savior has given you access into His presence (Heb. 10:19-23).

community

I don't know exactly how Jacob's reunion with Joseph happened, but I picture Jacob scanning the Egyptian horizon, waiting to be reunited with his son. Startled from his thoughts, a chariot emerged from beyond the horizon, its horses tearing toward him in haste. Who was this Egyptian royalty riding from on high in his direction? The image was fuzzy; time moved like quicksand. Finally a voice called out; the driver's horses were bridled. His chariot slid to a halt, and a man robed in Egyptian regalia leapt from his carriage and ran toward Jacob. And the son he once thought was dead appeared.

This was a divine moment to be sure. Jacob knew God had been in the business of appearing to His people, as we already noted today. Jacob had even encountered God's appearing to him at Luz and Beer-sheba. But all of these divine appearances were pointing to the ultimate appearing of God through the person of Christ. Paul, in his writings to Timothy and Titus, talked about Christ's first appearing and a second appearing that's to come.

READ 2 TIMOTHY 1:9-10.

Jot down everything Christ's appearing has accomplished for us.

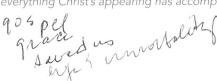

gospel
grace
saved us
life & immortality

TRUE/FALSE: *Our salvation is dependent on our good works (v. 9).* F

TURN A FEW PAGES FORWARD, AND READ 2 TIMOTHY 4:6-8. NOTE: PAUL IS NOW REFERRING TO JESUS' SECOND APPEARING.

From the tone of these verses, do you think Paul was afraid of Jesus' second coming or looking forward to it with great anticipation? Explain your answer based on the text.

Paul stated in 2 Timothy 4:8 that on the day of Christ's second coming, the Lord, our righteous Judge, would give Paul a crown of righteousness. Who else does Paul say will receive this crown? (Circle the best answer below.)

Those who are sinless
Those who showed courage
Those who loved/longed for His appearing
Those who did a lot of good

CLOSE BY READING TITUS 2:11-14.

What two appearances does Paul write about in this brief section?

cross, Mark

As Jacob stood on the foreign soil of Egypt, wrapped up in the arms of his son Joseph, I imagine nothing could have been more of a blessing to him than his son's appearing. Given the divine significance of the word *appear*, I can't help but think of a future reunion that is still to come: The appearing of Jesus as triumphant King. He won't be robed in Egyptian regalia but in the glory of God. He will wrap us in His arms, but instead of weeping, He will wipe every tear from our eyes. "Death will be no more; grief, crying, and pain will be no more, because the previous things have passed away" (Rev. 21:4b).

DAY 2
EXALTED TO SERVE

GENESIS 46:31–47:12

We've heard quite a bit about the land of Goshen over the past few days of our study. Historians aren't exactly sure what part of Egypt Goshen was located in, but it was likely in the northeast part of the Nile delta.[2] The area was well watered and the pastureland abundant for raising cattle.[3]

BEGIN TODAY BY READING GENESIS 46:31–47:6.

How did Pharaoh describe the land of Goshen in Genesis 47:6?

TRUE/FALSE: *The Egyptians had a special fondness for shepherds in their culture.*

How did the Egyptians' view of shepherds end up benefiting Jacob's family?

best Land

Pharaoh went above and beyond Joseph's request to settle his family in Goshen by offering to put them in charge of his livestock. Joseph's faithful and loyal track record with Pharaoh paved the way for his family's favored status.

PERSONAL REFLECTION: How does the way you walk out your relationships in faithfulness, integrity, and kindness benefit those coming behind you?

Judah was the one who went ahead of the family to help reunite Joseph with their father, but Joseph had the plan for how the family was going to survive in Egypt. By instructing his brothers to tell Pharaoh they were shepherds, Joseph helped them secure a spot in the pasturelands of Goshen. Because the Egyptians detested shepherds, Pharaoh put them in an area all by themselves. (This is like when I bring Mexican food onto an airplane and nobody wants to sit next to me. Winning!) Judah and Joseph both played roles in preserving and leading the family, and each of their roles would continue to grow in significance.

CONTINUE READING, IN GENESIS 47:7-12.

How old was Jacob when he met Pharaoh?

In what way did Jacob describe the years of his life?

I really love Jacob for this moment. He's a true melancholy if ever there was one. When Pharaoh politely asked his age, trying to break the ice and get the conversation rolling a bit, Jacob was basically like, "Well, I haven't lived nearly as long as everyone else who mattered in my ancestry. And every day has been pretty miserable and worthless and evil. So how are you doing, Pharaoh?" The King James Bible translation records Jacob's response as, "few and evil have the days of the years of my life been" (Gen. 47:9). Where were the essential oils and antidepressant herbs in Egypt? Get this man to the spa.

This picture of God's favor offers profound hope for any of us who, at a low point, might have characterized our lives in much the same way.

Strikingly, God was about to give Jacob some more years and turn some of that hardship into lavish blessing. This picture of God's favor offers profound hope for any of us who, at a low point, might have characterized our lives in much the same way. God was in the process of redeeming those difficult years.

When Joseph presented his father, Jacob, to Pharaoh, who blessed whom? (Circle the correct answer below.)

Pharaoh blessed Jacob   Joseph blessed Pharaoh

Jacob blessed Pharaoh   Pharaoh blessed Joseph

PERSONAL TAKE: Briefly look back at Genesis 12:3. How did this portion of God's covenant with Abraham influence Jacob blessing Pharaoh?

Here we find a fresh reminder that we're to bless those who don't share our faith, and certainly when they've been a help to us. Colossians 4:5-6 says, "Act wisely toward outsiders, making the most of the time. Let your speech always be gracious, seasoned with salt, so that you may know how you should answer each person."

PERSONAL RESPONSE: Who do you know who's not yet a follower of Jesus Christ? How can you specifically bless him or her?

REREAD GENESIS 47:11-12.

Below list all the things Joseph did for his family.

Joseph showed kindness to Pharaoh (outside his family and culture) and also to those inside his family.

PERSONAL RESPONSE: Think of someone in your spiritual or biological family who is hard for you to love. How can you show love to that person? Be specific.

Verses 11-12 are unexpected, undeserved, and altogether wonderful. They're the destination Joseph's dreams have been pointing to all these years—dreams over which the brothers were furious, dreams for which they hated Joseph. "'Are you really going to reign over us?' his brothers asked him. 'Are you really going to rule us?'" (Gen. 37:8a). Even Jacob rebuked Joseph over his dream. Part of their jealousy and anger was a result of their failure to understand the purpose of a ruler in God's kingdom. Throughout the Old Testament, God's leaders were to accomplish God's purposes for the sake of His people. I can't imagine Joseph understood all this when he first dreamed those dreams, but now we all finally see it: Joseph's rise to power wasn't for his own pride or prosperity—rather it was for his and his family's salvation and redemption, not to mention the salvation of future generations. The very one the family resisted was the one who would save them, settle them in the best land, and provide for them and their families.

TURN TO MATTHEW 20:20-28.

How were Jesus' followers to look exceedingly different from the Gentile rulers?

How does Jesus define greatness here?

It would have been Jesus' absolute right to call His followers to be servants while He reigned on an earthly throne. But Jesus calls us to be the very thing He was—a servant. He didn't use His authority to crush people or get ahead. He didn't look for people to serve Him, rather He looked for ways He could serve people. And, still, the most overwhelming piece of it all is that Jesus died a shameful death on a cross so He could give His life as a ransom for us.

PERSONAL RESPONSE: Each of us has a sphere of authority, whether in our homes, workplaces, or ministries. How are you using your place of authority to serve others? Be specific about the ways you can use your influence and resources to benefit the people around you.

Returning to our place in Genesis 47, we can't close today's study without reflecting on the irony of Joseph's position as second-in-command of Egypt. Earlier in their lives, Joseph's brothers despised the thought of him becoming their ruler. Many years later, it was the best news they could have ever hoped for.

PERSONAL TAKE: What do you think made the difference?

At first, the brothers resisted Joseph because they didn't understand he would be a ruler who rescues. We tend to think of rulers who oppress, step on the little people, or are simply out for their own good. But Jesus, far superior to our beloved Joseph, is a rescuing Ruler. He came to rescue us from enslavement to sin, and He has prepared a place for us to dwell in His presence when we pass from this life. But sometimes we forget that He came to give us abundant life on this earth, too! Are you resisting God's rule in your life? I've resisted Him at times. Sometimes I've thought He was out for my detriment instead of my well-being. Sometimes I've thought His reign in my life would be crushing, not life-giving. But God's rule is always for our good because His ways are trustworthy, loving, and righteous.

I CAN'T THINK OF A MORE FITTING PASSAGE FOR US TO CLOSE TODAY'S STUDY WITH THAN PHILIPPIANS 2:1-11. SLOWLY READ THROUGH THIS PASSAGE.

As you consider the purpose of Joseph's rise to power, one of servanthood and redemption, how does Jesus Christ perfectly exemplify the idea of being a leader who serves and rescues others?

Instead he emptied himself by assuming the form of a servant, taking on the likeness of humanity. And when he had come as a man, he humbled himself by becoming obedient to the point of death—even to death on a cross.

Philippians 2:7-8

PERSONAL RESPONSE: If you're resisting God in an area of your life, surrender to Him today. Tell Him you want to walk in obedience to Him. He wants to settle you in the best land. In New Testament terms, that's the place of abiding in His presence and the goodness of His will.

DAY 3

JOSEPH AND THE EGYPTIANS

GENESIS 47:13-26

Every time we open the Bible we're making a cross-cultural journey.

As I've mentioned before, every time we open the Bible we're making a cross-cultural journey, and it's not always to the same place. Sometimes we travel to the bustling city of first-century Corinth, other times to Nehemiah's 450 BC Jerusalem, or, like today, the land of ancient Egypt. Assuming we could actually visit those locations in their day, the unfamiliar geography and customs alone would be culturally confusing enough. How much more so when removed from these cultures by thousands of years? I'm sure you can tell by my very diplomatic introduction that we're in for a challenging read today. That said, I feel confident our minds will be stretched and hopefully our hearts will be enlarged after studying today's text.

READ GENESIS 47:13-26.

Besides the land of Egypt, what other land was experiencing severe famine? (It's mentioned three times in vv. 13-15. Remember the author of Genesis deliberately repeats what's important.)

PERSONAL TAKE: Why do you think the author makes this deliberate mention of the other famine-stricken land?

Today the focus of our story line changes from Joseph's relationship with his father and brothers to Joseph's relationship with the _____. (Circle the best answer below.)

Canaanites   Jebusites   Israelites   Egyptians

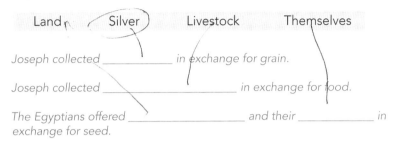

To better see the progression of the famine and what was required of the Egyptians for survival, fill in the blanks below with the appropriate answers from the following word bank. (Some of your Bible translations may differ slightly from this language, but the answers should be clear.)

Land   Silver   Livestock   Themselves

Joseph collected _____ in exchange for grain.

Joseph collected _____ in exchange for food.

The Egyptians offered _____ and their _____ in exchange for seed.

TRUE/FALSE: *Pharaoh was the one who profited off the Egyptians, not Joseph. (See vv. 14,20.)*

TRUE/FALSE: *Joseph didn't collect everything they owned all at once, but instead he took only what was needed in the moment for their survival.*

PERSONAL TAKE: Based on verses 23-25, how would you describe the Egyptians' response to Joseph's arrangement? In other words, did they feel good or bad about it? *good*

"You have saved our lives," they said. "We have found favor with our lord and will be Pharaoh's slaves."

Genesis 47:25

I don't think there's any way around the fact that Joseph set up a system in Egypt that included a form of slavery to Pharaoh. Grappling with this as modern-day Americans, and more importantly as Christians, it's helpful to keep a few things in mind. First, the Egyptians were grateful for Joseph's offer, telling him that he'd saved their lives and expressing they'd found favor with him (Gen. 47:25). Scholar Derek Kidner states, "It was axiomatic [self-evident] in the ancient world that one paid one's way so long as one had anything to part with—including, in the last resort, one's liberty."[4] This practice is shockingly different from the American mind-set, to be sure, where freedom is our country's middle name.

We also see that the Egyptians proposed the idea of selling themselves and their land to Joseph (v. 19); Joseph didn't suggest the idea. And since the Egyptians' livestock would have all died in the famine, you could argue that Joseph's purchase of cattle for food gave them something useful for what wouldn't have served them anyhow. The same thing goes for Joseph purchasing their land, which at that time could bring them nothing of sustenance. It's interesting to note that the 20 percent harvest tax was quite a bit lower than what was required in other ancient Near Eastern regions, so it appears Joseph acted generously with what he allowed the Egyptians to keep for themselves.[5]

We're also told that the profits from the arrangement went to Pharaoh, not to Joseph, so it wasn't as if Joseph personally profited from the agreement.

One commentator suggested, "Although we cannot know from Genesis, there is reason to believe that the voluntary submission of the people assumes that the enslavement was not permanent."[6] Lastly, "Although Joseph acknowledges that he 'bought' the people and their land for Pharaoh (v. 23), what follows is an informal agrarian pact, not treatment of the people as chattel (vv. 24-25). Since they agree to the proposal (v. 25), the arrangement is close to tenured farming, meaning that the farmer has access to the land and its produce and makes an agreed return to the owner."[7]

In short, all of the aforementioned realities don't erase the troubling system of the Egyptians being enslaved to Pharaoh and the fact that Joseph meted it out. But they do serve as helpful windows into how the starving Egyptians viewed Joseph's plan and into Joseph's heart as an overseer. He was a steward, not a tyrant, a sustainer of life, not a profiteer.

LOOK BACK AT GENESIS 41:33-36.

I believe God had many purposes for raising up Joseph during the seven years of abundance and seven years of famine. What reason is specifically stated in verse 36? That the land not perish

PERSONAL REFLECTION: As you consider the plight of the Egyptians in a desperate famine and God's goodness toward them through Joseph, what does this reveal about God's heart for the "outsider"?

When the Egyptians came to Joseph in Genesis 47:25, they said,

"You have _____ saved _____ our lives."

I am moved by the storehouses of grain God saved for a nation that didn't worship Him or follow His ways. God raising up Joseph to bring grain both to Canaan and Egypt gives us a glimpse of what was to come on a much grander scale in John's Gospel.

READ JOHN 6:22-35.

Why were the crowds looking for Jesus (v. 26)?

TRUE/FALSE: *Jesus spoke of two types of food: food that perishes and food that lasts for eternal life (v. 27).*

Who gives the food that lasts for eternal life (v. 27)? God

How does Jesus describe Himself in verse 35?

"I am the *bread* of life."

Come to Him, for He has come to you.

Though scholars may debate Joseph's methods in his dealings with Egypt, one thing is clear—God used him to save the Egyptians' lives. Surely the surrounding nations would have known about such a great salvation. As I think of Joseph and his grain that saved the Egyptians I can't help but think of the Bread of life who would one day give His very body and blood for all the nations of the world. "For the bread of God is the one who comes down from heaven and gives life to the world" (John 6:33).

Sometimes we consider the eternal bread found in Jesus as something less than the physical forms of bread we often set our hearts and affections on. We look to temporal pleasures to satisfy the hunger of our souls. But in reality the Bread of life is infinitely more precious and desirable than the bread that spoils. If you're hungry, hopeless, powerless, or in the middle of a famine, the storehouses of God in Jesus Christ are abundant and accessible. Come to Him, for He has come to you.

DAY 4

JACOB'S
FAITH REQUEST

GENESIS 47:27-31

Today we turn our attention back to an important moment in Jacob's life. In his youth, Jacob was a bit of an unscrupulous, sometimes deceiving, sort of character. In the years after losing Joseph he appeared tired and a little forlorn. (Peppy and zealous people don't describe their lives as short and unbearably hard.) Jacob's wearied disposition makes today's reading especially meaningful for at least two reasons.

First, after many years of fleeing from the storm he'd brewed in his family, scheming with his uncle for more money and cattle, wrestling with God, and losing his beloved son, regardless of how worn-out Jacob might be, God was still keeping His promise to him—Jacob would be blessed and made into a great nation. God's covenant wasn't dependent on how much faith or the lack of faith Jacob had on a given day—which somewhat ironically leads us into the next meaningful portion of today's reading. Jacob will finally exhibit some serious faith. The shiny, bedazzling treasures of Egypt that would have likely trapped Jacob earlier in his life were of no use to him now. God, His people, and His promises were all that Jacob was living for—and it had only taken him approximately 147 years to get here.

READ GENESIS 47:27-31.

By what name does the author refer to Jacob in verse 27? Israel

We've alluded to Jacob's two names before, but today we're going to briefly look at how and when he went from Jacob to Israel.

READ GENESIS 32:24-32.

Who renamed Jacob? God

What explanation is given for why Jacob was renamed Israel?

This section of Genesis is important to our study because it foreshadows who Jacob's family will become. In Genesis 47:27, when the narrator specifically says Israel settled in Goshen, he's speaking about both Jacob as an individual and his descendants who would blossom into the nation of Israel.

How did Jacob's family fare in the land of Egypt?
(Circle the best answer below.)

They acquired property.
They became fruitful.
They became numerous.
All of the above.

You may have noticed in our reading today we've suddenly moved to the end of Jacob's life, skipping approximately seventeen years. The Egyptians have been saved from the famine, and Jacob's entire family has more than survived it—they've thrived in it. Ironically, they've multiplied in Egypt while the Egyptians became slaves to Pharaoh in their own land. While the blessing and provision Jacob's family experienced in Egypt was astounding, we can't forget how jarring this move from Canaan to Egypt must have been for the family—foreign gods, religion, customs, and landscape. But it seems those issues might have been the least of Jacob's worries.

LOOK BACK AT GENESIS 17:1-8.

How did the current location of Jacob and his family seem to be at odds with God's covenant with Abraham (v. 8)?

"For my thoughts are not your thoughts, and your ways are not my ways." This is the LORD's declaration. "For as heaven is higher than earth, so my ways are higher than your ways, and my thoughts than your thoughts."

Isaiah 55:8-9

Imagine the complexity of Jacob's situation. God had clearly led Jacob and his family to Egypt. He was blessing and providing for them within that land, but Egypt wasn't the place He'd promised to Abraham's (and by extension Jacob's) family. Jacob surely wondered if they would ever get back to Canaan. If they were to get back, how in the world would it happen?

READ ISAIAH 55:8-9 AND ROMANS 11:33-36.

These verses are set in the context of God's surprising compassion and forgiveness toward us. Still, the general principle about God's unsearchable ways applies to what we've looked at today in Genesis.

PERSONAL RESPONSE: How do these verses give you confidence in God's leading, even when you don't understand His ways?

I've recently wondered what God was doing in my own life. Some exciting opportunities I was sure were going to happen didn't pan out; some disappointments I never saw coming came. Despite the chronic peculiarities in circumstances that should have gone off without a hitch, the consistent roadblocks have felt oddly orchestrated. As if God knows something I don't, as if He has a plan that's not my plan. (I may need Jacob's 147 years to get this.)

LET'S RETURN TO GENESIS 47:27-31.

How many years did Jacob live in Egypt? 17

PERSONAL REFLECTION: This is the same amount of years Jacob shared with Joseph earlier in his life. What does this unexpected and significant number of years tell you about the good and ordered hand of God in both their lives?

As Jacob neared the end of his life, what did he request Joseph do and not do for him? bury / take him in Canaan / don't bury him in Egypt

List all the reasons you can think of for Jacob to bring his request to Joseph instead of any of the other sons.

> *The longer I follow Jesus, though, the more the temporal pleasures of this earth really do dim in comparison to the joy of His fellowship.*

PERSONAL TAKE: Why do you think the place where Jacob was buried was so important to him? (Remember what you read today in Genesis 17:1-8.)

I love what Waltke says about this: "Jacob pins his hope and destiny on the land promised to the fathers, not on Egypt's abundance."[8] "To the end, Jacob remains committed to the faith of his fathers, expressed by his commitment of his body to the Promised Land. He is not bamboozled by prosperity in Egypt."[9]

To use Waltke's word, I've been bamboozled by the shiny objects of what money can buy, hoodwinked by the allure of fame, swept up by dynamic personalities that weren't always authentic. The longer I follow Jesus, though, the more the temporal pleasures of this earth really do dim in comparison to the joy of His fellowship and the privilege of loving and serving people, pleasures that are eternal. The end of

Jacob's life inspires me to live fully in view of God's promises, even the ones that might be a way off. Jacob could have made his permanent home in Egypt and identified with its prosperity, but he knew that none of those flash-in-the-pan riches could hold a candle to taking his place as part of God's royal lineage. Jacob would return to Canaan, even if just his bones made the trip.

TURN TO HEBREWS 11 AND READ VERSES 8-10,13-14.

Abraham, Isaac, and Jacob saw God's promises _____.
(Circle the best answer below.)

At night   Close up
From a distance   In a dream

PERSONAL TAKE: Abraham, Isaac, and Jacob all lived in temporary and moveable tents. What does this tell you about how they viewed their lives on earth?

What were they ultimately looking for (vv. 10,14)?

PERSONAL REFLECTION: In light of these verses in Hebrews, describe how the faith of the patriarchs might look today. In other words, what would it look like to live with that same faith in our modern times?

Jacob finally knew what mattered. Even though he could only see the promises from afar, Jacob joined God in His promise, determined to return to Canaan even if it was for his burial. The promised land was not ultimately about the physical land of Canaan, rather it was pointing to an eternal city whose builder and maker is God.

PERSONAL RESPONSE: What's one temporal pursuit that's taking up a significant amount of your time and attention? How can you take back some of that time for something that will matter for eternity? (The eternal could be investing in a relationship, serving a neighbor, teaching a class, taking a class, greeting at church, making a meal for someone, or starting a prayer group, just to name a few options.)

Genesis 47:31b says, "Then Israel bowed in thanks at the head of his bed." Translators have difficulty knowing whether this passage refers to Jacob worshiping God or bowing in deference to Joseph. If it's the latter it would correspond with the second of the two dreams, where even Jacob bowed down before Joseph.[10] If this is correct, I'm again struck by the reality that something Jacob rebuked Joseph for—having a dream where Jacob would bow down to Joseph—had turned out to be a joyful, spiritual blessing for Jacob. He was not resentfully or reluctantly bowing down before Joseph, rather he was willingly and gratefully doing so, for Joseph would enable Jacob to return to the burial place of his forefathers. The ways of God we so often resist, once again, prove to be the paths of life.

The ways of God we so often resist, once again, prove to be the paths of life.

DAY 5

THE DOUBLE PORTION

GENESIS 48:1-12

I wonder if sometime during this study you've let yourself start hoping again. Maybe you gave up a long time ago on a promise the Lord gave you. If you're like me, when God kindles a vision in your soul you eagerly fan the oxygen of God's Word and faith-filled prayers onto its burgeoning flame. Sometimes the flame grows into a crackling fire beyond your imagination, and other times the flame is extinguished by betrayal, loss, illness, or just plain life. When disappointment happens, our hopes can evaporate as surely as embers give way to thin swirls of smoke. We snuff out the dream from our memories and go on our way. As the dream goes, so goes some of our hope and faith.

Sometimes dreams have to die for God to resurrect them.

What we forget, or simply don't realize, is that sometimes dreams have to die for God to resurrect them. Even if a flame goes out, it's no match for a God who can relight it—and, yes, I do love a pun. As we continue to see God fanning His covenant promise to the patriarchs (Abraham, Isaac, and Jacob) into flame, be encouraged by the renewed hope God gave individually to Jacob and Joseph in our study. Yes, God was keeping His promise to Abraham, future Israel, and future nations, but don't miss for a second that while doing so He also lifted the hopeless head of Jacob, reviving his soul! He redeemed Joseph's story and would double his blessing. Dear friend, if the promise God has given you is in accordance with His Word and will, you keep hanging on. He's not out of matches.

READ GENESIS 48:1-12.

PERSONAL REFLECTION: What part of this passage is most meaningful to you? Why?

When Joseph set out to visit his father after hearing Jacob was close to death, who did Joseph bring with him?

What surprising turn of events happened in verse 5?

Jacob said sons were his

PERSONAL TAKE: Given that Manasseh and Ephraim's mother was an Egyptian (Gen. 41:50), does Jacob's adoption of his grandsons surprise you? Why or why not?

Your two sons born to you in the land of Egypt before I came to you in Egypt are now mine. Ephraim and Manasseh belong to me just as Reuben and Simeon do.

Genesis 48:5

When Joseph's Egyptian wife gave birth to his sons in the land of Egypt, I can't imagine Joseph ever dreamed a moment like this was possible— that he would see his father again, that his sons would meet their grandfather, and most improbable, that Jacob would adopt Joseph's sons as though they were his own. This adoption didn't mean Jacob would raise them—he was at the very end of his life. It meant they would be full recipients of the divine inheritance granted to Jacob's family, as if Manasseh and Ephraim were Jacob's own firstborn and second-born, like Reuben and Simeon. Jacob would bestow his blessing on his two grandsons in exactly the same way he was about to bless his actual sons. Jacob had fifty-three grandsons, and Joseph's sons were the only two elevated to the level of sons (Gen. 46:7-27).

PERSONAL REFLECTION: When you think of the loss and hardship in Joseph's life, what does this unexpected blessing of his sons' elevated status tell you about God's redemptive heart?

SLOWLY TAKE IN VERSES GENESIS 48:3-4 AGAIN.

Before Jacob explained his adoption of Manasseh and Ephraim, he recounted the time God appeared to him in Bethel (Luz) in the land of Canaan. In doing so, Jacob let Joseph know he had the authority to do what he was about to do. (Though God was with Joseph, there's no biblical record of Him ever appearing to Joseph the way He did to Abraham, Isaac, and Jacob.) This is kind of like when you were growing up and your mom told you to do something, and you asked, "Why?"

And then she gave you the universal reason, "Because I'm the mom."

Here, Jacob says, "Because God appeared to me."

Compare Genesis 35:11-12 with Genesis 48:3-4 and complete the exercises below:

TRUE/FALSE: *In both accounts, God is referred to as God Almighty.*

In chapter 35, God tells Jacob that part of his legacy will include _____, though Jacob's statement in chapter 48 does not mention it. (Circle the best answer below.)

Tribes   Land   Possessions   Kings

PERSONAL TAKE: In Genesis 35:11, God told Jacob to "be fruitful." In 48:4, Jacob recalled Him saying, "I will make you fruitful … " The first statement is in the imperative form; the second reads like a promise God would fulfill. Why do you think Jacob recounted it the way he did?

When Jacob spoke of the land God promised to him and his future descendants, he was referring to the land of Canaan. Why did this now seem impossible?

No matter how seemingly impossible, Jacob was going all-in on the promise of God, the promise that one day his descendants would return to and inherit the land of Canaan. And by God's authority, Joseph's legacy wouldn't miss out on that inheritance even though Joseph was sold into slavery in Egypt by the evil actions of his brothers. His legacy, in fact, would double as Manasseh and Ephraim would be counted as Jacob's sons.

Look back at Genesis 48:7. Why do you think Jacob brought up his wife Rachel's death here?

This mention of Rachel's death in Bethlehem while giving birth to Benjamin seems out of the blue. It's helpful to note Jacob was probably explaining since he only had two sons by his beloved wife Rachel, Joseph and Benjamin, God was now adding to that number by giving him Manasseh and Ephraim, too.[11]

When Jacob, who was nearly blind, asked about the boys Joseph brought with him, Joseph responded, "They are my sons God has given me here" (v. 9). Notice that simple word *here*—here, as in the land of Egypt. Joseph's confident proclamation that God had given

God's redemption is able to cross borders and restore what seems hopelessly lost.

him two sons in the land of Egypt, by an Egyptian wife, is profound. How beautiful and hopeful for all of us: no matter how distant the place we find ourselves in, how unorthodox or unexpected our situations are compared to what we think they should be, God's redemption is able to cross borders and restore what seems hopelessly lost.

PERSONAL REFLECTION: Look back at verse 11. Name one thing God has done for you that you never expected. Briefly write about it below.

Western Wall
Twins

This week we've overturned a few more pieces to the puzzle, and God's covenant promise has come into clearer focus. My earnest prayer is for God Himself—His mercy, redemption, power, blessing, and love—to have also become more radiant to you. Perhaps my favorite thing about all that we've studied this week is Jacob's recollection of God's words to him in Bethel, "I will make you fruitful and numerous ... " (Gen. 48:4). No doubt Jacob set out to accomplish the charge God had given him—to be fruitful and multiply. But all these years later, on his deathbed, Jacob realized his life's vast fruit and multiplication had been brought to pass as a result of God's doing, not his own.

PERSONAL RESPONSE: We close our week being reminded that we serve a God who always keeps His promises to us. What promise of God are you currently dismissing or disregarding? What change do you need to make in your life in order to live as though that promise is true?

NOTES

SESSION 7 VIEWER GUIDE

A REDEMPTION STORY

Redeem - to reclaim as one's own -
to buy back.

GROUP DISCUSSION

What portion of the video teaching really resonated with you? Why?

How does God's redemptive work in Joseph's story point to the redemptive work of Christ in the New Testament?

How does God's amazing redemption in Jacob and Joseph's lives encourage you to keep praying for redemption in situations that appear irredeemable?

Is there a promise from God's Word that you're close to giving up on? How has Joseph's story encouraged you to keep walking, believing His promises are true?

A redemption story is only possible with a Redeemer. Jacob described God as having been a Shepherd to him. How has He proven to be a Shepherd to you?

Who in your sphere of influence needs to know the Redeemer? How are you making the love of Jesus known to him or her?

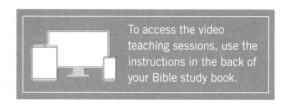

To access the video teaching sessions, use the instructions in the back of your Bible study book.

Simple Sausage Casserole

(serves 6)

INGREDIENTS

1 (16-oz) package ground sausage

Cooking spray or butter

5–6 cups 1-inch bread cubes, plain white
   sliced bread or Italian bread slices,
   crust discarded

1½ cups shredded mozzarella cheese

¾ cup shredded cheddar cheese

6 eggs

¾ cup heavy cream

¾ cup milk

I included recipes in my first Bible study because my friends who helped me with that first manuscript and I shared many meals together. We wanted to share those meals with you. Since then I've realized there's no turning back. I'm always keeping my eyes open for accessible recipes that feed a group, taste good, and are moderately healthy. This one may not meet the healthy standard, but it's over-the-top in taste.

DIRECTIONS

Brown sausage in a large skillet over medium heat, breaking apart with a wooden spoon. Set aside.

Grease a 13x9-inch casserole dish and set aside. In a large bowl, combine the bread cubes, sausage, and cheeses. Mix well and transfer to the casserole dish.

In a separate bowl, whisk the eggs with heavy cream and milk. Pour the egg mixture over the bread mixture. Cover with plastic wrap and refrigerate overnight.

When you're ready to bake the casserole, preheat your oven to 350 degrees. Discard the plastic wrap, and bake uncovered for 35 minutes or until golden brown and set. Let stand 10 minutes before serving.

A FAITHFUL FINISH

My dad has always been an avid walker. Between our neighborhood strolls together when I was younger and our hikes on vacation, taking walks has evolved into one of my favorite pastimes. I'm trying to pass on this healthy and relational activity to my seven-year-old nephew, Will, and six-year-old niece, Harper, in hopes of creating meaningful experiences with them like the ones I had with my dad. (My niece Lily is only two, so her time is coming.)

I may have been overly zealous in pursuit of this noble endeavor the day I talked Will and Harper into walking with me around a nearby lake. Its surrounding landscape is thickly wooded with mature trees, and it's home to deer, turtles, and an interesting variety of birds. It's one of our favorite places to visit. However, walking the entire lake trail was apparently more than they bargained for. They lamented how their feet hurt, how their legs suddenly weren't working, and how enormous this lake was, as though it had swelled into the Mediterranean Sea. "Aunt Kelly," Harper moaned, "Can we just turn around? I'm so tired!"

Turning around would have been a reasonable possibility except that we'd already crossed the halfway mark. Continuing forward was obviously the quickest route back, but try explaining that to a fatigued first grader. (I'm sincerely convinced that while Harper is at elementary school learning how to spell the word *elephant*, she's also preparing to take the bar exam—she was kindly and respectfully arguing me into a pretzel.) The last half of our hike consisted of her relentlessly trying to persuade me to turn around and me trying to convince her that moving forward was the fastest way home. Oh the irony!

Harper's flawed perception of the best way forward wasn't lost on me. I've let a faulty viewpoint like this mislead me in life on more than hikes. As followers of Christ it can sometimes feel like we're moving in the wrong direction, completely contrary to what our internal compasses tell us. We determine that if we want to get home we best turn around. But if anything stands out to me about Joseph's life it's that while he seemingly started out in the wrong direction, toward Egypt, Joseph never left the trail of God's purpose. And more importantly, God never left his side. As we close our study it is only fitting that, by the grace and sovereignty of God, the circuitous route of Joseph's life would eventually be the one to lead him home.

DAY 1
THE UNEXPECTED BLESSING

GENESIS 48:13-22

I wonder what life would have looked like for Jacob if as a teenager he could have somehow harnessed all the wisdom and clear perspective he had at the age of 147. But faith is typically forged through time, experience, and hardship. I suppose if faith came any easier it wouldn't be faith. In today's reading we'll find Jacob at the end of his life, rising up with humility, authority, and a God-given take-chargeness we haven't seen from him before. Jacob's faith budded in Bethel, grew in Haran, strengthened at the ford of Jabbok, faltered in Canaan at the loss of Joseph, and revived in Egypt. It would at last come into full bloom in his final days. By faith, Jacob would take hold of promises yet to come. I contend it will be his finest moment yet.

READ GENESIS 48:13-22.

Even though Jacob couldn't see Manasseh and Ephraim well, he was able to hold them in his arms. "I never expected to see your face again … , "Jacob said to Joseph, "but now God has even let me see your offspring" (v. 11). This right here is the lavishness of God. What Jacob couldn't have possibly imagined, seeing his son Joseph, God not only accomplished but also exceeded by allowing Jacob to see his two grandsons.

In our efforts to avoid the prosperity gospel, sometimes I think we go too far in thinking our God is a God of scarcity instead of the God He really is, the God of abundance. The Old Testament teems with examples of God's spiritual and physical blessings upon His people, as does the New Testament. Paul said, "And God is able to make every grace overflow to you, so that in every way, always having everything you need, you may excel in every good work" (2 Cor. 9:8).

PERSONAL REFLECTION: Take a moment to ponder this question: In what area of your life have you stopped believing in the abundance of God's presence and provision? How does Jacob's long wait for certain blessings encourage you that God has not abandoned or forgotten you?

> *Jacob took an unexpected action when blessing his grandsons (vv. 13-14). Joseph wanted his father to put his right hand on his oldest son,*
> _____.
>
> *Jacob insisted on putting his right hand on Joseph's youngest son,*
> _____.
>
> *According to Genesis 48:17-18, how did Joseph feel about Jacob's choice of blessing the younger over the older? (In verse 13, we also see Joseph guiding his sons in the opposite direction.)*

PERSONAL TAKE: Look up Hebrews 11:21. Why do you think the author of Hebrews mentioned Jacob blessing his grandsons as a significant act of faith?

> *Being open is especially challenging when it relates to our long and dearly held plans for ourselves and our loved ones.*

In ancient Israel, blessing the oldest son with a double inheritance was a custom called primogeniture. Along with this inheritance came headship of the family, property rights, and responsibility for the family, among other things.[1] Joseph would have been attached to the idea of his firstborn, Manasseh, receiving the double portion from Jacob. When Jacob put his right hand on Ephraim instead of Manasseh, this signified a major shift in Joseph's vision and plan for his sons.

My mom and I recently texted about a situation our family wouldn't have looked for or ever thought to pray for. She said, "God's ways aren't always our ways; I'm open." Being open is especially challenging when it relates to our long and dearly held plans for ourselves and our loved ones. But this humble posture of openness to God avails us to what God wants to bring us and loosens our grip on how we think things should go. It also acknowledges our trust in God and His sovereignty.

PERSONAL RESPONSE: Joseph had to get on board with God's choice of Ephraim as the one who would receive the double portion. Is there anything the Lord is doing in your life that you're not open to? Any plan you're holding so tightly that you're unwilling to move where God is blessing? Take some time to surrender this area to the Lord. He will never mislead you. (Preaching to myself today.)

Today's passage gives us a clear picture of God's sovereignty—He is not bound by customs, birth order, or people's expectations. Much like Isaac and Jacob receiving the blessing that customarily would have gone to their firstborn brothers (Ishmael and Esau, respectively), so Ephraim would be given the blessing he had no natural claim to. Similarly, a Savior would come through the line of Jacob many generations later to give His people what they could not attain. Jesus would bless the outcast and the undeserving (Matt. 5:1-12) and offer salvation for those who could never earn it—to you and to me.

Turn ahead to the New Testament and look up the following passages. How does each one speak to God's grace and the gift of relationship with God through Christ for those who can't earn it?

Romans 3:21-24

Ephesians 2:8-9

Ephesians 2:12-13,19-20

Turn back to Genesis 48:15-16. While Jacob's right hand rested on Ephraim and his left on Manasseh, Jacob described God based on some significant experiences he'd had with Him. Fill in the blanks below (your translations may vary slightly).

The God before whom his fathers Abraham and Isaac had _____.

The God who had been his _____ all his life.

The _____ who redeemed him from all harm.

WALKING WITH GOD

The Bible's description of the patriarchs having walked with God indicated their close relationship with Him, one that encompassed every facet of their lives. Jacob referenced Abraham and Isaac and

their intimate relationship with God, as a way of identifying himself with the God of his forefathers as well as attaching Joseph (and Ephraim and Manasseh) to Him.

According to Deuteronomy 30:15-16, what does walking with God look like?

The LORD is my shepherd; I have what I need.

Psalm 23:1

How does the prophet Micah describe walking with God in Micah 6:8?

GOD AS SHEPHERD

Consider Psalm 23:1-4. What does God do for His people as shepherd? In addition, think of anything you know about a shepherd's care for his flock.

How does Jesus fulfill the description of our Shepherd in John 10:11-18?

GOD AS PROTECTIVE ANGEL & REDEEMER

In Genesis 48:16, what did Jacob say the angel did for him?

Jacob characterized God as his delivering angel. Your translations may vary using the word *redeemed* or *delivered*. The Hebrew word is *goel*, and this is its first mention in the Bible. It means "the act of releasing or setting free."[2] This word is rich with meaning, ultimately foreshadowing the coming of Jesus Christ not only as one who redeems but also as our Redeemer.

How does Jesus fulfill the description of Redeemer in Titus 2:11-14?

I don't think Jacob could have imagined that one day the God of his fathers would send His Son to be both Shepherd and Redeemer for the world. When Jacob placed his right hand on Ephraim's head we learned that "receiving the blessing which God offers does not rest on natural status in the world. On the contrary, the blessings of God are based solely on God's grace. The one to whom the blessing did not belong has become heir of the promise."[3] In much the same way, the blessing of salvation did not belong to us, but now it is ours through Jesus Christ.

PERSONAL RESPONSE: If you have yet to surrender your life to Jesus Christ, our strong Shepherd and glorious Redeemer, pore over John 10:11-18 and Titus 2:11-14. Confess today your inability to save yourself from the sin that has separated you from God, and receive the divine blessing of being made right with Him through the death and resurrection of Jesus Christ. See the appendix on p. 213.

The blessings of God are based solely on God's grace.

At first blush Jacob blessing his two grandsons seems like a nominal scene in the story, yet the author of Hebrews cites it as one of Jacob's great moments of faith. When Jacob blessed Manasseh and Ephraim as his own sons, he was actively taking part in God's promise for nations to come from him. Jacob trusted God would fulfill what Jacob would not see come to pass. In laying his hands on the heads of his grandsons, Jacob was laying hold of God's promises.

PERSONAL RESPONSE: What step of obedience can you take in the "here and now" that's based on what God has promised in the "yet to come"?

One of the most challenging and exciting parts of the Christian life is walking in obedience to Jesus now, while not always knowing when or how God will fulfill His promises to us in the future. This is precisely what makes faith, faith. And it ever pleases Him (Heb. 11:6).

DAY 2

THE BLESSINGS OF THE TWELVE

GENESIS 49:1-28

God's promise to Abraham has continued to press forward.

I just watched my 22-month-old niece behold the wonder of Easter egg hunting for the first time. Spotting a pastel egg in the grass and breaking it open while a piece of candy tumbles out is a unique thrill. It was especially entertaining to watch her be utterly surprised every single time she opened a new one, as though each candy-filled egg was the first she'd ever seen. Studying Scripture can have a similar feel, its truths sometimes sitting in the shadows or tucked into obscure crevices. When we discover a meaningful insight in the Word, especially after diligently searching, the reward is invaluable. I pray this last week of studying the life of Joseph will hold certain surprises we've yet to see.

God's theme of blessing is central to the Book of Genesis. God blessed man and woman in the garden before sin entered the world, and He also blessed them after the fall. Despite sin wreaking havoc on relationships, destroying lives, and leaving the earth groaning under a curse, God's promise to Abraham—for land, descendants, and all the nations on earth to be blessed through him—has continued to press forward.

READ GENESIS 49:1-28.

We'll spend the bulk of our time studying Judah and Joseph's blessings, but we'll briefly look at the blessing of each son. Keep in mind these blessings focus on the tribes that will come from the sons as much as they are about the individual men. (The first six mentioned are Leah's sons.)

REUBEN

What did Jacob say would keep Reuben from excelling (v. 4)?

You can read more about Reuben's indiscretion in Genesis 35:21-22.

SIMEON AND LEVI

Simeon and Levi are paired together because of a violent incident they were both involved in. (You can read about it in Genesis 34.) What did Jacob especially take issue with in verse 6?

You might say the first three blessings are actually anti-blessings, and in a sense, they are. But considering Jacob's sons will ultimately form the twelve tribes of Israel, the fact that Reuben's sexual immorality and Simeon and Levi's unrestrained violence will not set the tone for the nation's leadership is a blessing for the nation as a whole.

JUDAH

PERSONAL TAKE: Do the positive prophecy and rich blessing for Judah and his descendants surprise you? Why or why not?

Verse 10 in the NIV says, "The scepter will not depart from Judah, nor the ruler's staff from between his feet, until he to whom it belongs shall come and the obedience of the nations shall be his."

> **TRUE/FALSE:** *The word* scepter *is a symbol of eminence and kingship. The kingdom ultimately belongs to someone who would come in the future.*
>
> **TRUE/~~FALSE:~~** *One nation will be obedient to this ruler.*
>   all nations
>
> *Turn to Matthew 1 and read verses 2-6. What renowned king will come from the line of Judah (v. 6)? (Circle your answer below.)*
>
> Moses   Joshua   David   Samuel
>
> *We already briefly touched on this on Day 1 of Session 6 (p. 129). According to Matthew 1:16, who came through the line of David?*

Genesis 49:11-12 contains several metaphors not apparently obvious to the modern reader.

The scepter will not depart from Judah, nor the ruler's staff from between his feet, until he to whom it belongs shall come and the obedience of the nations shall be his.

Genesis 49:10, NIV

- Tying up everyday animals to the best vines in the land is a picture of overwhelming abundance.[4]
- Aged wine as commonplace as water for washing clothes paints a picture of overflowing prosperity.
- Eyes darker than wine and teeth whiter than milk show the incomparable strength and power of this coming ruler.[5]

While the passage clearly points to King David's throne, we also see the promise of a messianic ruler who will sit on His throne and reign for eternity. Jesus will be a mighty warrior who will conquer death and restore peace and blessing. Sailhamer puts in nicely: " … Jacob had in view a kingship that extended beyond the boundaries of the Israelites to include other nations as well."[6]

PERSONAL REFLECTION: What does the promise of Jesus Christ coming through the unexpected line of Judah reveal about the grace of God?

Let's continue with a very brief survey of the rest of Jacob's sons, leaving Joseph for last. (Note: Issachar and Zebulun are Leah's fifth and sixth sons. Gad and Asher are the sons of Zilpah, Leah's maidservant. Dan and Naphtali are the sons of Bilhah, Rachel's maidservant. Benjamin is Rachel's son. I'm so glad you're never going to forget this.)

ZEBULUN, ISSACHAR, DAN, GAD, ASHER, NAPHTALI, BENJAMIN

Generally speaking, how do the blessings of these seven sons differ from the blessings of the three sons before Judah (Reuben, Simeon, and Levi)?

JOSEPH

We'll spend the rest of today considering the blessing of Joseph. "He who was once separated from his brothers through spite is now separated from his brothers by blessing."[7] Only God could have accomplished this.

REREAD VERSES 22-26.

How many times is a form of the word bless used in Joseph's section?

God is referred to in five different ways in verses 24-25. As you list each one in the spaces below, notice how central He is to the blessing of Joseph.

1.

2.

3.

4.

5.

Yet his bow remained steady, and his strong arms were made agile by the hands of the Mighty One of Jacob, by the name of the Shepherd, the Rock of Israel.

Genesis 49:24

Joseph is described as a fruitful vine whose branches climb over a wall. The expression is not easily translated but the gist is clear—Joseph's descendants will multiply greatly, as already indicated by Ephraim's name,[8] "God has made me fruitful in the land of my affliction" (Gen. 41:52b).

PERSONAL REFLECTION: Thinking back to the beginning of our study when Joseph was sold into slavery, none of us could have imagined Joseph's life flourishing under such horrible conditions. What do these blessings upon Joseph tell you about what God is able to accomplish in the midst of trials and hardship?

Throughout our study I've wondered how Joseph made it through the betrayal, loneliness, and separation from his family. How he was able to keep serving through the false accusations in prison and how he not only forgave his brothers but also lovingly sustained them through famine. The broad answer to these questions is found in the central, underlying theme of our study: *God was with him.* By now I hope we are all clear that we can do nothing apart from God (John 15:5). But God's presence with us can sound so familiar and general that we stop hearing its meaning. Notice in today's text the specific imagery used to represent God's presence in Joseph's life. It's stunning!

When "the archers" attacked him, what about Joseph remained steady and strong? How did this happen?

In the end we see, the only blessings that endure are the ones with which God Himself crowns us.

I'm struck by the obvious but deeply significant reality that God Almighty was the only one who could truly bless Joseph. Surely Joseph sought blessing from his father, Jacob, a blessing that came in the form of harmful favoritism and a multi-colored robe that attracted jealousy. Perhaps Joseph had wanted a blessing from Potiphar or Pharaoh, or maybe he'd always wished for it from his brothers. But in the end we see, the only blessings that endure are the ones with which God Himself crowns us.

PERSONAL RESPONSE: Are you seeking blessing from a person, thing, or experience? No person or earthly experience will come close to satisfying your deepest longings. Spend time confessing this to God, and ask Him to help you seek the gift of His presence and the blessings only He can bring.

Verse 25 says the Almighty blessed Joseph with "blessings of the heavens above" and "blessings of the deep that lies below." I don't know for sure all the author meant by this metaphor, but the first thing I thought of was how many "blessings of the deep" Joseph had known—blessings in a foreign land, blessings in temptation, blessings in a prison. When Jesus meets us in the deep places, we never forget His presence or His blessings there.

PERSONAL REFLECTION: Write about a "blessing from the deep" you never would have received from the Lord had you not gone through a difficult time.

If I had written the story, no doubt I would have chosen for the Messiah to come through Joseph's line instead of Judah's. But God's grace is on full display here. God sent a Savior through those and to those who don't deserve it. And He raised up Joseph to save a nation, a foreshadowing of Jesus' ultimate salvation. I hope we won't soon forget Genesis 49:10. The One to whom the kingdom belongs has come. His name is Jesus. He will come again, and all nations will be obedient to Him.

PERSONAL RESPONSE: In the space below, write out Philippians 2:9-11.

DAY 3
DEATH OF A PATRIARCH
GENESIS 49:29–50:14

I've missed Joseph the past several days of study. It seems our story, while soon returning to him, has shone its spotlight on some of the other characters in its cast. This reminds us that the grand narrative of Genesis isn't all about Joseph or all about Jacob, nor is it rising and falling at the hands of the brothers. The Book of Genesis, and the Bible for that matter, is ultimately about a loving Creator keeping His covenant promise to His people.

I want to live a life fueled by a faith that sees past the grave, grasping the promises that live beyond it.

Of course each person's character and choices still matter, as we saw in yesterday's study when each son received an appropriate and fitting blessing. Somehow God put the actions of every person to work, both the good and bad, moving His plan of redemption forward. I will never grasp the mystery of it all, but what I know is this: I want to live a life fueled by a faith that sees past the grave, grasping the promises that live beyond it.

READ GENESIS 49:29-33.

Jacob instructed his sons to bury him in a cave in the field of Machpelah. In what important land was this burial place located? (Circle the best answer below.)

Canaan   Goshen   Hebron   Bethel

Below circle the name of the person who was not buried in this cave:

Abraham   Sarah   Isaac   Rebekah   Rachel   Leah

Does it surprise you that Jacob would want to be buried next to Leah instead of Rachel? Why is this detail important? (Hint: Look back at yesterday's study on the significance of Judah's legacy, the legacy of Leah's son.)

You may remember from our first week of study, Jacob was tricked into marrying Leah. Jacob went through the obligation of Leah's bridal week so he could marry Rachel, the one he truly loved. Now at the end of his life, Jacob could have told his sons to lay him next to Rachel near

Bethlehem. He could have chosen to be buried in Egypt, the place he'd prospered with his family the past seventeen years, the place of his beloved son's reign. Instead, Jacob chose to be counted among his fathers in the place God had promised to each of them, an act of faith and quite remarkably an act of obedience. He finally understood God's calling is deeper than our plans, our dreams, and even our loves.

I thank God for the opportunities He's given me to choose Him and His ways over my personal desires, though it has never come easily. He has blessed my obedience with unexpected relationships, gifts, and opportunities. And where certain longings remain unmet, He is forging my faith and teaching me to live contentedly in the waiting.

God's calling is deeper than our plans, our dreams, and even our loves.

PERSONAL REFLECTION: How does Jacob's faith to identify with God's promises—even though they hadn't been fulfilled in his lifetime—encourage you to live fully in light of the eternal promises of Christ?

CONTINUE BY READING GENESIS 50:1-14.

Describe Joseph's response to his father's death (v. 1).

Joseph worked hard on his relationships with both his brothers and his father. While we have no biblical record of Joseph resenting his father for the favoritism that set Joseph up to be hated by his brothers, I can imagine his emotions toward Jacob were complex and layered. In any case, Joseph put a lot of effort and care into his family relationships whether the family members deserved it or not. Joseph's emotion at Jacob's death displayed his deep affection.

PERSONAL REFLECTION: How does Joseph's strong tie to his father inspire you to work hard at your most significant relationships?

What unexpected people group also mourned over Jacob's death (v. 3)?

List everyone who went to Canaan for Jacob's burial (vv. 7-8).

What other people group witnessed the mourning ceremony (v. 11)?

By now you're well acquainted with the three elements of God's covenant with Abraham: God would give Abraham and his descendants **land**; his descendants would grow into a great **nation**; all nations of the earth would be **blessed** through him (Gen. 12:1-3). *All nations.* The groups who witnessed Jacob's burial were significant: his Hebrew descendants, the Egyptian officials, and the Canaanite inhabitants all took part. The nations were witnessing the mighty hand of God.

PERSONAL TAKE: Very few details are given about Abraham's death (Gen. 25:7-11) and Isaac's death (Gen. 35:27-29). Why do you think we're given so many specific details surrounding Jacob's death and burial? Give this some thought.

The elaborate picture of Jacob and his sons returning temporarily to the promised land accompanied by the Egyptian army foreshadows the further fulfillment of God's covenant with Abraham. Let's briefly look at what happened approximately four hundred years after Jacob's death, when a new Pharaoh was in power, a Pharaoh who knew nothing of Joseph and who despised the Israelites.

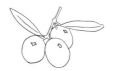

READ EXODUS 1:8-14.

One of Pharaoh's complaints about the Israelites was their enormous and increasing size. How was Israel's size significant to God's covenant with the nation of Israel?

And God heard their groaning; and God remembered his covenant with Abraham, with Isaac, and with Jacob.

Exodus 2:24

READ EXODUS 2:23-24.

What did God remember when he heard the Israelites' groaning?

God raised up a leader named Moses to deliver the Israelites out of slavery in Egypt (Ex. 3). After substantial resistance, the Lord brought the Israelites through the Red Sea on their way to the promised land of Canaan.

READ EXODUS 14:21-30.

What similar details are given in Genesis 50:9 and Exodus 14:23? Yet how are the circumstances significantly different?

The future nation of Israel would have noticed the irony of the high officials of Egypt, their horses and chariots, accompanying Jacob's sons back to Canaan to bury Jacob. This image "would have brought to mind the salvation of God at the Red Sea."[9] But for Joseph and his brothers, this was a long way off—an event they wouldn't see in their lifetimes.

PERSONAL TAKE: Look back at Genesis 50:14 from today's text. In light of God's promise to bring Israel back to Canaan, do you think Joseph felt he was going in the wrong direction? Why or why not?

PERSONAL REFLECTION: What does Joseph's journey from Canaan back to Egypt tell you about God's timing? What does it tell you about living faithfully in the place God has you now while still clinging to His promises?

Today was a full day of study. You've done such a thorough job exploring the many layers of Joseph's story and tracing God's promises through it all. As we close today, two things are clear at Jacob's death: his desire to be counted among the people of God and his faith that God's promises would prevail, namely, that his descendants would inherit the land of promise.

PERSONAL RESPONSE: Specifically, how do Jacob's instructions about his burial inspire you to live a life fully committed to God and His promises, even when the fulfillment of those promises seems far off?

DAY 4
FORGIVENESS AND DIVINE PERSPECTIVE

GENESIS 50:15-21

Joseph's complex relationship with his brothers runs like a thread from Genesis 37 to the end of the book. Just when you think that thread has disappeared into a family fabric of trust and serenity, the needle pokes back into their present. Though our trying relationships can get wearisome, there's something to be said for the sanctification that happens in us as a result of their exasperating nature. I've experienced some of the deepest heart transformation in the context of difficult relationships, especially when I've allowed them to mold me into the image of Christ. That's the tidy way of putting it—I'm not saying it's always pretty.

On this second to last day of *Finding God Faithful* our story will return to Joseph and his brothers, the people with whom we started, and to the God who's been bringing about redemption all along.

READ GENESIS 50:15-21.

Joseph's brothers thought he might retaliate after their father's death. What does this reveal about their misunderstanding of Joseph's heart toward them?

Why do you think the brothers had trouble receiving—or believing in—Joseph's kindness, love, and forgiveness toward them over the past seventeen years?

PERSONAL REFLECTION: Why do you have trouble receiving forgiveness either from others or from God?

Why do you think Joseph wept when he learned about his brothers' fear of his revenge, thinking he hadn't forgiven them?

The CSB translates "Jacob's message" on behalf of his sons, "Say this to Joseph: Please forgive your brothers' transgression and their sin—the suffering they caused you" (v. 17). The Hebrew words used here for *transgression* and *sin* paint the strongest image of sin.[10] Joseph's brothers understood their actions against Joseph were evil and horrifying; they also came to understand that these actions were sins against God. After acknowledging their sin to Joseph by way of sending the message, they threw themselves down before him in humility. If ever a perfectly satisfying picture of a guilty party at the feet of the innocent existed, this scene of the brothers remorsefully begging for forgiveness would be it.

Perhaps you've thought the only way you could forgive your offender was if he or she were to fall down before you, own his or her sin, and plead for mercy. But Joseph took no joy in his brothers' wallowing before him as slaves. Actually, this episode had no bearing on his forgiveness toward them. **Joseph's emotional response toward his brothers showed he'd forgiven them long before that moment.**

PERSONAL REFLECTION: If Joseph's forgiveness wasn't based on what his brothers had or hadn't done, what was it based on?

If you've been afraid to draw near to God because of your sin, don't let fear stop you from coming to Him.

REREAD GENESIS 50:19.

Of all the things he could have said, Joseph told his brothers not to be afraid. Have you ever been afraid as a result of your own sin? Maybe it was fear over the consequences? Fear over your sin being known? Fear over what your sin revealed about you as a person? In this moment, Joseph reflected the gracious and merciful heart of God toward sinners. If you've been afraid to draw near to God because of your sin, don't let fear stop you from coming to Him. As New Testament believers in Jesus Christ, His death and resurrection open the way for us to draw near to Him "in full assurance of faith" (Heb. 10:19-22).

What place or role did Joseph not assume (Gen. 50:19)?

Joseph understood that he was not the Judge. He directed his brothers' attention away from himself and toward God, knowing the limits of his authority. One of the fundamental elements of forgiving others is realizing we're not in the place of God. When we forgive a person who's wronged us, we're placing the situation and outcome in God's hands. I can't help but think of 1 Peter 4:19, "So then, let those who suffer according to God's will entrust themselves to a faithful Creator while doing what is good." Joseph could forgive his brothers because he'd already entrusted himself to his faithful Creator, the One who knows hearts, the only One capable of judging righteously. And on top of that, he'd embraced God's perspective on his difficult circumstances.

In the space below, write out Genesis 50:20.

One of the fundamental elements of forgiving others is realizing we're not in the place of God. When we forgive a person who's wronged us, we're placing the situation and outcome in God's hands.

In many ways, Genesis 50:20 is the crux of the Joseph story. This passage by no means calls evil by another name, nor does it sweep harm and abuse under the rug of denial or head-in-the-sand oblivion. Joseph's statement is a head-on acknowledgement that evil exists in the world, and far more personally, that it existed against him. At the same time we find a parallel track of God's goodness and redemption, not running in place of evil, but somehow running alongside it, with God ultimately having His way with evil in the end.

PERSONAL RESPONSE: Is there someone you've yet to forgive? Are you holding onto bitterness and anger? Put it before the Lord. Entrust yourself to Him. Trust that His plan of goodness for you hasn't failed. Forgive. Write your words of forgiveness in the space below.

According to verse 20, what ultimate purpose did God accomplish through His good plan for Joseph?

PERSONAL REFLECTION: I don't know what hardships you've traversed or what paths your life has taken you down. As you reflect on how God used Joseph's story for the redemption of many people, how do you see God using your unique life and story for the blessing of others?

You planned evil against me; God planned it for good to bring about the present result—the survival of many people.

Genesis 50:20

IT'S ONLY FITTING TO CLOSE TODAY BY READING ROMANS 8:28.

What do both Genesis 50:20 and Romans 8:28 tell us about what God can do in any situation?

"You planned evil against me; God planned it for good …" (Gen. 50:20a). That word *good* is reminiscent of the way the Book of Genesis began. John Sailhamer makes the connection, "Behind all the events and human plans recounted in the story of Joseph lies the unchanging plan of God. It is the same plan introduced from the very beginning of the book, where God looks out at what he has just created for humanity and sees that 'it is good' (1:4-31). Through his dealings with the patriarchs and Joseph, God had continued to bring about his good plan. He had remained faithful to his purposes, and it is the point of this narrative to show that his people can continue to trust him and to believe that 'in all things God works for the good of those who love him, who have been called according to his purpose.' (Rom. 8:28)."[11]

I hope this study has helped you see the bigger picture of God's story of redemption through Joseph's story. In Genesis, God's plan for creation was good and His faithfulness to His people trustworthy. This remains true today.

PERSONAL REFLECTION: How has a deeper understanding of God's plan of redemption through Joseph's story helped you more clearly see what He is doing today? How does this understanding affect you personally and the way you choose to live?

DAY 5
FINALLY HOME
GENESIS 50:22-26

Starting a Bible study of any kind requires courage and commitment. And coming to the end of one is best tied up with a ribbon of reflection. So my prayer is that you'll take the opportunity over the next few days to consider the truths you've learned from God's Word and the ways you can faithfully serve the Lord whether you're in the pit or the palace. I hope you'll never forget one of the things evidenced in Joseph's life: people who fail you can't prevent God's plan for you.

I'm so thankful for your perseverance in finishing this study. I will never be able to fully put into words what an honor it is to walk alongside you through my written and spoken words. It's one of the most fulfilling privileges of my life. I only wish I could hear your personal testimonies of how God is interacting with you based on Joseph's story and ultimately how you're *Finding God Faithful* through it all.

PERSONAL REFLECTION: Before we get to today's reading, what's the single most impacting truth or insight you've experienced in this study?

People who fail you can't prevent God's plan for you.

READ GENESIS 50:22-26.

Based on Genesis 37:2 and 50:22, approximately how many years did Joseph live in Egypt?

We don't know how old Joseph was when Jacob moved his family to Canaan from Paddan-aram, but we do know Joseph lived most of his years outside the land of promise.

LOOK AT GENESIS 39:2-3,21,23.

What recurring phrase is mentioned? How did this reality make all the difference for Joseph while living in a foreign land?

We experience His ultimate gift in His presence with us.

Throughout this study, I've been consistently reminded of a concept we began with: The God of promise is even better than the land of promise. That's not to say God's somehow disconnected from His promises. Rather, as we wait for certain promises to be fulfilled, we experience His ultimate gift in His presence with us.

According to Joseph, what would God eventually do for his people (v. 24)?

Hebrews 11 is often referred to as the Hall of Faith. In this chapter, the author mentions many well-known people from the Old Testament and the specific ways they exhibited faith in their lifetimes. Joseph's mention in the Hall of Faith is succinct and somewhat surprising.

READ HEBREWS 11:22.

By faith, what two things did Joseph do? I filled the first one in for you.

1. He spoke about (mentioned) the exodus of the Israelites out of Egypt.

2.

Out of all the moments of faith Joseph could have been noted for, I initially found the author of Hebrews's choices interesting. How about, *by faith Joseph continued to follow God despite being sold into slavery in Egypt? By faith, he obeyed God and didn't sleep with Potiphar's wife? By faith, he served God while in prison? By faith, he stockpiled grain for seven plentiful years in light of God's promise of famine? By faith, he gave his two sons Hebrew names, despite having long been living in Egypt? By faith, he forgave his brothers?* I don't think the author of Hebrews would disagree with me—these were all acts of faith on Joseph's part. But none of these made the "big two."

PERSONAL TAKE: Why do you think the author of Hebrews chose to highlight these two acts of faith?

In Genesis 50:24 Joseph says, "I am about to die, but God … " *But God* is one of the most powerful pairings of words we'll ever find in Scripture. Even though Joseph had been the savior of his family, the protagonist of a rags-to-riches story, and an impeccable picture of godliness, death was at his door. He'd taken his family—and the future nation of Israel—as far as he could take them. In reality, God was the One who'd carried the family, and God would be the One to continue the story that has been His all along.

Joseph told his fellow Israelites that God would eventually bring them out of Egypt and into Canaan "not because he had experienced it, but because God had promised it."[12] And that, I do believe, is the definition of faith.

PERSONAL REFLECTION: What have you yet to experience that God has promised in Scripture? How are you living in light of that promise despite having yet tasted it?

Joseph made his people promise, when God came to their aid and moved them back to Canaan, to take his bones from Egypt and bury him in the land promised to Abraham, Isaac, and Jacob. Much like Jacob's action, Joseph chose to identify himself with the place of God over and above the place of his prosperity. **By faith, he wanted to be counted among the people of God.**

Hundreds of years later, after Moses, God would raise up a leader named Joshua to take the people of Israel into the promised land.

READ JOSHUA 21:43-45.

What had never failed?

READ JOSHUA 24:32.

PERSONAL REFLECTION: What does this verse tell you about God's faithfulness to us?

READ JOSHUA 24:1-13.

These passages give us a helpful summary of Israel's story, beginning with Abraham up to the point of the Israelites coming into the land. It's encouraging to reflect on all God did, even when it seemed at times He'd lost control of the story.

PERSONAL REFLECTION: How has studying Joseph's life and God's covenant with His people bolstered your confidence in God's faithfulness? Try to draw from a specific truth from our study together.

She conceived and bore a son, and she said, "God has taken away my disgrace."

Genesis 30:23

Hebrews 11:13 reminds us that the patriarchs "... all died in faith, although they had not received the things that were promised." Joseph took hold of the promises of God as though they were his present reality, as though they were as tangible as the Egyptian sand beneath his feet. But his was not a blind faith. It was faith alright, make no mistake. But it was a faith rooted in a relationship with the God who was with him, the God who had never left him and would see his bones not only to Canaan, but also his resurrected body to the heavenly Jerusalem (Heb. 12:22).

PERSONAL REFLECTION: Joseph lived and died by faith in God. What fear or attachment is still holding you back from taking a step of faith in your relationship with Jesus? Write a prayer of surrender to the Lord in the space below.

As we bring our study to a close, I'd like you to look up Genesis 30:23, a verse you may remember from the beginning of our study. When Rachel held Joseph in her arms, what did she say God had taken away from her?

Considering Joseph's story in light of God's covenant with Abraham helps us uncover a deeper meaning. When God made His covenant with Abraham, Abraham didn't know how the story would unfold. He only knew what had been promised, and he knew his God was able. When Rachel gave birth to Joseph, Abraham's grandson, and proclaimed that God had taken away her disgrace (reproach) through the precious gift of her son, little did she know, one day another Son would be given who would take away the sin of the world.

Even as we come to the end of Joseph's story we're not coming to the end of God's. When Joseph's relatives placed him in a coffin in

Egypt, God was still writing His narrative. As Joseph predicted, God eventually came to the aid of His people and delivered them from Egypt into the promised land of Canaan—those who came to Egypt as Jacob's fledgling family left as the nation of Israel. God prospered them and patiently persevered with His people in Canaan even though they consistently wavered back and forth between obedience and rebellion. When Israel blatantly rejected God as their King and begged for a human king, God gave them what they asked for in King Saul and his disappointing reign. Eventually Samuel anointed God's chosen man for the job, King David. (As you know from our study, King David was a descendant of Judah, Jacob's son.)

Many generations came and went before the promised Messiah, the eternal King, was finally born in Bethlehem through the line of David. Indeed, Jesus was born a King but a totally different kind of king than Israel or the world had ever seen. He came to save His people from their sins (Matt. 1:21). He came to bear our shame on the cross (Heb. 12:2), and in so doing, He removed our disgrace and clothed us in His righteousness instead (2 Cor. 5:21). He conquered death through His resurrection (1 Cor. 15:20-22). The blessing that came to Joseph through the God of Abraham, Isaac, and Jacob has now come to us in all its fullness through Jesus Christ.

I have loved studying the life of Joseph with you, and can't help but end where we began:

> You know, then, that those who have faith, these are Abraham's sons. Now the Scripture saw in advance that God would justify the Gentiles by faith and proclaimed the gospel ahead of time to Abraham, saying, All the nations will be blessed through you. Consequently those who have faith are blessed with Abraham, who had faith … Christ redeemed us from the curse of the law by becoming a curse for us, because it is written, Cursed is everyone who is hung on a tree. The purpose was that the blessing of Abraham would come to the Gentiles by Christ Jesus, so that we could receive the promised Spirit through faith.

GALATIANS 3:7-9,13-14

God raised up Joseph to save a family, and He lifted up His Son to save the world. What a beautiful story it is, one no one could have written but God.

SESSION 8 VIEWER GUIDE

A FAITHFUL FINISH

GROUP DISCUSSION

What portion of the video teaching really resonated with you? Why?

Joseph's brothers were unable to shatter the dream God had given him, and no one can shatter the purposes God has for you. How does Romans 8:28 encourage you to keep loving and following God, confident He will accomplish His purposes in your life?

How do the small daily choices we make contribute to our faithful finishes? How can you pay more attention to those seemingly small things?

What has God put on your heart to do that has lay dormant in your life for some time? What is keeping you from stepping out in obedience?

How have you seen God turn something meant for evil into something good? How did this deepen your trust in Him?

If you've suffered through brokenness, how can you live in light of God's sovereignty and goodness, rather than wallow in the wrong done to you? (What side of the semicolon are you living on?)

What's been the most meaningful truth you've learned about God in this study?

To access the video teaching sessions, use the instructions in the back of your Bible study book.

#FINDINGGODFAITHFUL

Berry Trifle (serves 6–8)

INGREDIENTS

Custard:

1 (14-ounce) can sweetened condensed milk

2 cans milk (Use the empty sweetened
    condensed milk can to measure.)

4 egg yolks

¾ teaspoon vanilla

2 tablespoons cornstarch

1 (8-ounce) can table cream (I prefer Nestle.)

Whipped Cream:

2 cups whipping cream

Berries and Cake:

4 tablespoons sugar

2 cups strawberries

2 cups blueberries

1 cup raspberries

1 cup blackberries

1 pound cake, cut into 1-inch squares
    (Homemade or store-bought)

Garnish: Fresh mint leaves

DIRECTIONS

To make the custard: In a medium saucepan, over medium heat, whisk together sweetened condensed milk, milk, egg yolks, vanilla, and cornstarch. Whisk constantly, cooking until the custard thickens into the consistency of a pastry cream. Pour the custard into a bowl, and add the table cream. Mix well and cover with plastic wrap, pressing the plastic wrap directly onto the surface of the cream to avoid forming a skin. Place in refrigerator to cool.

To make whipped cream: Place the whipping cream in a large bowl or stand mixer. Whip until the cream produces soft peaks. Set aside.

To make the berries: Mix the sugar and all of the berries in a large bowl. Let the berry mixture stand for 30 minutes to bring out the juices of the fruit.

To assemble the trifle: Begin with a layer of custard in the trifle bowl. Then add a layer of cake, followed by a layer of the berry mixture and 3 tablespoons of fruit juice. Next add a layer of whipped cream. Repeat. Once the final layer of whipped cream is at the top of the trifle bowl, garnish with some berries and mint leaves. Refrigerate completed trifle for at least one hour before serving.

ADAPTATIONS: You can also make mini-trifle desserts using individual cups instead of a large trifle bowl. In that case, lady fingers (2 packages broken into 2-inch pieces) may be substituted for the pound cake.

This is one of Regina's signature dishes. Regina is a dear friend, gifted chef, and my co-conspirator on my cookbook, *A Place at the Table,* where you'll find this recipe along with other delicious and nourishing recipes. Bring this Berry Trifle to a gathering, and you'll be the belle of the ball.

Leader Guide
INTRODUCTION

Finding God Faithful: A Study on the Life of Joseph is a video- and discussion-based Bible study as part of The Living Room Series. The weekly personal study along with the teaching videos will promote honest conversation as you study Scripture together. Since conversation is essential to the experience, you'll find a few starter questions in both the Viewer Guides and the following Leader Guide to help get the discussion rolling.

It's our hope that the added recipes will encourage groups to eat together because so many great friendships and conversations naturally begin around a dinner table. That said, this study may be used in a variety of large or small group settings including churches, homes, offices, coffee shops, or other locations.

Each week you'll show a video teaching. You'll find detailed information on how to access the videos on the card inserted in the back of the Bible study book. If your group doesn't have adequate Internet connection for video streaming, DVD sets are available for purchase at lifeway.com/findinggodfaithful. That is where you will also find promotional tools and other helpful resources.

TIPS ON LEADING THIS BIBLE STUDY

PRAY: As you prepare to lead *Finding God Faithful*, remember prayer is essential. Set aside time each week to pray for the women in your group. Listen to their needs and the struggles they're facing so you can bring them before the Lord. Though organizing and planning are important, protect your personal time of prayer before each gathering. Encourage your women to include prayer as part of their own daily spiritual discipline as well.

GUIDE: Accept women where they are, but also set expectations to motivate commitment. Be consistent and trustworthy. Encourage women to follow through, engaging with the personal study on the study, and attend the group sessions. Listen carefully, responsibly guide discussion, and keep confidences shared within the group. Be honest and vulnerable by sharing what God is teaching you throughout the study. Most women will follow your lead and be more willing to share and participate when they see your transparency. Reach out to women of different ages, backgrounds, and stages of life. This diversity is sure to enrich your conversation and experience.

CONNECT: Stay engaged with the women in your group between group meetings. Call, text, email, use social media, or send a quick note in the mail to connect with them and share prayer needs throughout the week. Let them know when you are praying specifically for them. Root everything in Scripture and encourage women in their relationships with Jesus.

CELEBRATE: At the end of the study, celebrate what God has done by having your group share what they've learned and how they've grown. Pray together about what further steps God may be asking you to take as a result of this study.

TIPS ON ORGANIZING THIS BIBLE STUDY

TALK TO YOUR PASTOR OR MINISTER OF EDUCATION OR DISCIPLESHIP: If you're leading this study as part of a local church, ask for your leaders' input, prayers, and support.

SECURE YOUR LOCATION: Think about the number of women you can accommodate in your designated location. Reserve tables, chairs, or media equipment for the videos, music, and additional audio needs.

PROVIDE CHILDCARE: If you are targeting moms of young children and/or single moms, childcare is essential.

PROVIDE RESOURCES: Order the needed number of Bible study books. You might purchase a few extra for last minute sign-ups.

PLAN AND PREPARE: Become familiar with the Bible study resource and leader helps available. Preview the video sessions and prepare an outline based on the leader helps available to aid you as you lead the group meetings.
Visit *Lifeway.com/FindingGodFaithful* to find free extra leader helps and promotional resources for your study.

EVALUATE

At the end of each group session, ask: What went well? What could be improved? Did you see women's lives transformed? Did your group grow closer to Christ and to one another?

NEXT STEPS

Even after the study concludes, follow up and challenge women to stay involved through another Bible study, church opportunity, or anything that will continue their spiritual growth and foster friendships. Provide several ministry opportunities for members to participate in individually or as a group. These ministry opportunities will give women a chance to apply what they have learned through this study.

SESSION 1

1. Welcome group members to the study and distribute Bible study books.

2. Watch the Session 1 teaching video.

3. Following the video, lead participants through the Group Discussion section of the Session 1 Viewer Guide (p. 9).

4. Close the session with prayer.

SESSION 2

1. Welcome group members to Session 2

of *Finding God Faithful*. Use the following questions to review the previous week's personal study.

Which day of personal study meant the most to you? Why?

Why is it important to set the context for this study by reviewing God's covenant with Abraham?

How did favoritism wreak havoc in Joseph's family? How did the Scriptures from Day 3 help you deal with jealousy so it doesn't hinder your own relationships?

Joseph would wait many years before God fulfilled his dreams, yet God was with him in his waiting. How are you currently experiencing Christ's presence as you actively wait on Him for your own longings to be fulfilled?

How are you already seeing God orchestrating events in the life of Joseph? How does this give you confidence that He's working in your most difficult circumstances?

How did Joseph respond when God seemed to be working contrary to Joseph's understanding of God's plan? How do you respond in similar situations?

How do you see the faithfulness of God in this week's study?

2. Watch the Session 2 teaching video, encouraging group members to take notes as Kelly teaches.

3. Following the video, lead participants through the Group Discussion section of the Session 2 Viewer Guide (p. 36).

4. Close: Lead a time of prayer, thanking God for His sovereignty, acknowledging everything is under His authority and in His control. Tell Him you trust Him for all things, in all seasons of life.

SESSION 3

1. Welcome group members to Session 3

of *Finding God Faithful*. Use the following questions to review the previous week's personal study.

Which day of personal study meant the most to you? Why?

Why was Joseph especially vulnerable to temptation? At what times are you most vulnerable to temptation?

How has God used suffering to make you fit for future kingdom work?

Have you ever felt forgotten by God? Explain. How does God's presence with Joseph in difficult circumstances reorient your thinking about His presence with you in challenging times?

Certain blessings can only come in the midst of difficulty. How have you experienced God's blessings in the midst of your struggles?

Joseph had an impossible task. Is there a God-given task you currently feel inadequate to accomplish? How can you specifically draw on Christ's strength during this time? Explain.

On Day 4 we looked at several verses about putting our trust in God and not in people or our resources. Share a time when you found God faithful after everything and everyone else had failed you.

2. Watch the Session 3 teaching video, encouraging group members to take notes as Kelly teaches.

3. Following the video, lead participants through the Group Discussion section of the Session 3 Viewer Guide (p. 64).

4. Close: Provide a time of prayer for those who may be going through a season of suffering. You may choose to lead a prayer for the whole group or spend time praying for each person walking through a difficult time.

SESSION 4

1. Welcome group members to Session 4

of *Finding God Faithful*. Use the following questions to review the previous week's personal study.

Which day of personal study meant the most to you? Why?

What did you learn about the Holy Spirit from this week's study?

God put Joseph in a position of power to lead and bless others. How are you using your past experiences, current season of life, and resources for God's kingdom work?

Joseph named his son Ephraim, meaning "God has made me fruitful in the land of my affliction." (See Gen. 41:52.) What does this tell us about the relationship between blessing and hardship?

God stewarded Joseph's hardships, readying him for the tasks ahead. How have you seen God steward your hardships?

Joseph served God in prison and palace. Do you find it easier to serve God in times of abundance or times of want? Explain.

How can you proactively (and lovingly) stand out as salt and light in your sphere of influence?

In what ways do you see God faithfully working through a famine to bring about the reunion of Joseph and his brothers?

2. Watch the Session 4 teaching video, encouraging group members to take notes as Kelly teaches.

3. Following the video, lead participants through the Group Discussion section of the Session 4 Viewer Guide (p. 92).

4. Close: Lead a brief brainstorming time to gather ideas of how the group members might bless others out of their abundance. This could be a one-time service project or an ongoing ministry. Select some participants to help put feet to the idea. Close with prayer, thanking God for His abundance in your lives.

SESSION 5

1. Welcome group members to Session 5 of *Finding God Faithful*. Use the following questions to review the previous week's personal study.

Which day of personal study meant the most to you? Why?

How did Joseph's brothers interpret the difficulties they were facing? Based on our study, how can you tell the difference between God's discipline in your life and a trial that has nothing to do with your sin?

God was leading Joseph's brothers on a path of repentance. What has this week's study taught you about God's discipline and the gift of repentance (Rom. 2:4)?

When all the brothers bowed before Joseph it signaled the fulfillment of one of his dreams. What does this scene teach us about God's sovereignty and how His plans for us aren't thwarted by those who oppose us?

As Joseph moved his brothers from fear of punishment to peace around his table, how has Jesus brought you from a place of fear to one of peace?

So far, what wisdom have you gleaned from the ways Joseph dealt with his complex and difficult family relationships?

What evidence convinced Joseph the hearts of his brothers had changed? Share one significant thing Jesus has changed about you since coming to know Him.

2. Watch the Session 5 teaching video, encouraging group members to take notes as Kelly teaches.

3. Following the video, lead participants through the Group Discussion section of the Session 5 Viewer Guide (p. 120).

4. Close: Enlist one of the participants to close the session by praying for group members to have courage and compassion as they extend mercy to others in the same way Christ extended mercy to them.

SESSION 6

1. Welcome group members to Session 6 of *Finding God Faithful*. Use the following questions to review the previous week's personal study.

Which day of personal study meant the most to you? Why?

Why does the story of Judah and Tamar appear in the middle of Joseph's story?

What did you learn from this story about God's grace and His ability to bring good out of the darkest situations? How does this minister to you?

What are the characteristics of a repentant heart? How did Judah display them?

How does Joseph forgiving his brothers sit with you? Are you overwhelmed by the grace displayed or conflicted that the brothers didn't get what was coming to them? Let the forgiveness we've experienced from Jesus serve as the backdrop for the discussion.

What helped Joseph reach a place of forgiveness? How can these same things aid you in forgiving those who have hurt you?

How do Joseph's actions point toward the redemption Christ offers us?

2. Watch the Session 6 teaching video, encouraging group members to take notes as Kelly teaches.

3. Following the video, lead participants through the Group Discussion section of the Session 6 Viewer Guide (p. 150).

4. Close: For some in your group, seeking forgiveness or granting forgiveness will be a very difficult step. Provide a quiet moment for participants to pray about taking this action.

Encourage them to pray alone or with a fellow group member.

SESSION 7

1. Welcome group members to Session 7 of *Finding God Faithful*. Use the following questions to review the previous week's personal study.

Which day of personal study meant the most to you? Why?

What moves you the most about Joseph's reunion with Jacob? When have you experienced a sweet reunion with a long lost friend or family member? How do you see the faithfulness and grace of God in this reunion?

Name all the ways Joseph used his place of authority to benefit the people around him. How can you become more of a servant leader?

Describe a time when God did something in your life that initially baffled you, but later you realized His purpose far exceeded your expectations.

What temporal pursuit is currently taking up too much of your time and attention? How can you shift focus to pursue something of eternal value?

How do God's fulfilled promises to Jacob encourage you to remain faithful in following Jesus? Be specific.

What have you learned about Jesus through the Old Testament story of Joseph?

2. Watch the Session 7 teaching video, encouraging group members to take notes as Kelly teaches.

3. Following the video, lead participants through the Group Discussion section of the Session 7 Viewer Guide (p. 178).

4. Close: Divide participants into smaller groups, and encourage each group to spend time interceding for those they know who don't

know the Redeemer.

SESSION 8

1. Welcome group members to Session 8 of *Finding God Faithful*. Use the following questions to review the previous week's personal study.

Which day of personal study meant the most to you? Why?

God blessed Joseph and his family abundantly. In hardships we can sometimes mistakenly believe God is a God of scarcity not abundance. How does Joseph's story challenge this thinking?

Practically speaking, what does it mean for you to walk with God? How would you assess your current walk with Him?

What step of obedience do you need to take right now based on what God has promised you in His Word?

How do you see the grace of God at work in the Messiah's being born through Judah's line?

How has studying God's faithfulness to Joseph and the people of God strengthened your confidence in God's faithfulness, especially as it relates to the gift of Jesus?

What key truths are you taking away from this study? How will you apply these truths to your life?

2. Watch the Session 8 teaching video, encouraging group members to take notes as Kelly teaches.

3. Following the video, lead participants through the Group Discussion section of the Session 8 Viewer Guide (p. 206).

4. Close: Wrap up the study by encouraging participants to share key truths they're taking away from the study. Be sure to discuss how they will apply what they've learned. Share your gratitude for their participation, and offer a prayer of blessing over your group as you close.

BECOMING A CHRISTIAN

Romans 10:17 says, "So faith comes from what is heard, and what is heard comes through the message about Christ."

Maybe you've stumbled across new information in this study. Or maybe you've attended church all your life, but something you read here struck you differently than it ever has before. If you have never accepted Christ but would like to, read on to discover how you can become a Christian.

Your heart tends to run from God and rebel against Him. The Bible calls this *sin*. Romans 3:23 says, "For all have sinned and fall short of the glory of God."

Yet God loves you and wants to save you from sin, to offer you a new life of hope. John 10:10b says, "I have come so that they may have life and have it in abundance."

To give you this gift of salvation, God made a way through His Son, Jesus Christ. Romans 5:8 says, "But God proves his own love for us in that while we were still sinners, Christ died for us."

You receive this gift by faith alone. Ephesians 2:8-9 says, "For you are saved by grace through faith, and this not from yourselves; it is God's gift—not from works, so that no one can boast."

Faith is a decision of your heart demonstrated by the actions of your life. Romans 10:9 says, "If you confess with your mouth, 'Jesus is Lord,' and believe in your heart that God raised him from the dead, you will be saved."

If you trust that Jesus died for your sins and want to receive new life through Him, pray a prayer similar to the following to express your repentance and faith in Him:

> "Dear God, I know I am a sinner. I believe Jesus died to forgive me of my sins. I accept Your offer of eternal life. Thank You for forgiving me of all my sins. Thank You for my new life. From this day forward, I will choose to follow You."

If you have trusted Jesus for salvation, please share your decision with your group leader or another Christian friend. If you are not already attending church, find one in which you can worship and grow in your faith. Following Christ's example, ask to be baptized as a public expression of your faith.

ENDNOTES

SESSION 2

1. James A. Swanson, *A Dictionary of Biblical Languages with Semantic Domains: Greek (NT)* (Oak Harbor: Logos Research Systems, 1997).
2. Jeannine K. Brown, *Scripture as Communication* (Grand Rapids, MI: Baker Academic, 2007), 226.
3. Robert D. Bergen, *The New American Commentary, Volume 7, 1–2 Samuel* (Nashville, TN: B&H Publishing Group), 70.
4. Ibid, Swanson.
5. Kenneth A. Mathews, *The New American Commentary, Volume 1B—Genesis 11:27–50:26* (Nashville, TN: Broadman & Holman Publishers, 2005).
6. Ibid.
7. Ibid.
8. Beth Moore (@BethMooreLPM), Tweet, January 5, 2019, https://twitter.com/BethMooreLPM/status/1081564014277214209.

SESSION 3

1. Gordon J. Wenham, *Word Biblical Commentary, Volume 2, Genesis 16–50* (Dallas, TX: Word Books, 1994).
2. Ibid, Mathews.
3. Ibid.
4. Ibid.
5. Ibid.
6. Hugh C. White, *Narration and Discourse in the Book of Genesis* (Cambridge: Cambridge University Press, 1991), 256.
7. Ibid.
8. Derek Kidner, *Tyndale Old Testament Commentaries, Volume 1, Genesis* (Downer's Grove, IL: InterVarsity Press), 204.
9. Ibid, 205.
10. "Definition of tsaraph," *Blue Letter Bible* https://www.blueletterbible.org/lang/lexicon/lexicon.cfm?Strongs=H6884&t=CSB, accessed on March 24, 2019.
11. C. H. Spurgeon, *The Treasury of David* (Grand Rapids, MI: Kregel Publications, 1968). Retrieved from https://app.wordsearchbible.com, accessed on March 25, 2019.
12. "Definition of Zaaph" *BibleHub.com* https://biblehub.com/hebrew/2196.htm, accessed on March 26, 2019.
13. Ibid, Mathews.
14. Ibid.
15. Ibid.
16. "Definition of ruwts," *Blue Letter Bible* https://www.blueletterbible.org/lang/lexicon/lexicon.cfm?Strongs=H7323&t=CSB, accessed on March 26, 2019.
17. "Lexicon for Genesis 41:16," *Bible Hub* https://biblehub.com/interlinear/genesis/41-16.htm, accessed on March 26, 2019.
18. "Definition of Ra,'" *Bible Hub* https://biblehub.com/hebrew/7451.htm, accessed on March 26, 2019.
19. John H. Sailhamer, *The Pentateuch as Narrative: A Biblical-Theological Commentary* (Grand Rapids, MI: Zondervan, 1992), 214.
20. Ibid, 215.

SESSION 4

1. Ibid, Mathews.
2. Irving Cohn and Frank Silver, "Yes, We Have No Bananas" (1923). Vocal Popular Sheet Music Collection, Score 1777.
3. "Definition of Ecclesiastical," Merriam-Webster.com, accessed on May 21, 2019.
4. John Stott, *The Message of the Sermon on the Mount* (Downer's Grove, IL: InterVarsity Press, 1978).
5. Ibid, Mathews.
6. Ibid.
7. Ibid, Sailhamer, 218.

SESSION 5

1. Bruce K. Waltke with Cathi J. Fredricks, *Genesis: A Commentary* (Grand Rapids: MI, Zondervan, 2001), 547.
2. John H. Walton, *The NIV Application Commentary: Genesis* (Grand Rapids, MI: Zondervan, 2011), 661. Retrieved from https://app.wordsearchbible.com, accessed on May 2, 2019.
3. Robert E. Longacre, *Joseph: A Story of Divine Providence, A Text Theoretical and Text Linguistic Analysis of Genesis 37 and 39–48* (Winona Lake, IN: Eisenbrauns, 2003), 47.
4. Ibid, Walton.
5. Ibid, Mathews.
6. Ibid, Waltke, 556.
7. Ibid, Mathews.
8. Ibid, Longacre.
9. "Definition of expiatory," Merriam-Webster.com, accessed on May 22, 2019.
10. W. E. Vine, Vine's Expository Dictionary of New Testament Words, *Blue Letter Bible*

https://www.blueletterbible.org/search/dictionary/viewTopic.cfm?topic=VT0002239, accessed on April 8, 2019.
11. Horatio G. Spafford, "It Is Well with My Soul," *Baptist Hymnal* (Nashville, TN: Lifeway Worship, 2008), 447.

SESSION 6

1. Ibid, Sailhamer, 209.

2. Edward J. Woods, *Tyndale Old Testament Commentaries, Volume 5, Deuteronomy: An Introduction and Commentary* (Westmont, IL: InterVarsity Press, 2011), 257. Retrieved from https://app.wordsearchbible.com, accessed on May 21, 2019.
3. Ibid, Waltke, 508.
4. Ibid, Sailhamer, 221.
5. "Definition of Right," *Blue Letter Bible* https://www.blueletterbible.org/lang/lexicon/lexicon.cfm?Strongs=H6663&t=CSB, accessed on April 9, 2019.
6. John Newton, "Amazing Grace" 1779. https://library.timelesstruths.org/music/Amazing_Grace/, accessed on May 22, 2019.
7. Ibid, Sailhamer, 221.
8. Ibid, Waltke, 566.
9. Ibid, Swanson.
10. Ibid, Mathews.
11. Ibid, Waltke, 559.
12. Ibid, Mathews.
13. Ibid, Waltke, 573.
14. Ibid, Waltke, 574.
15. Ibid, Waltke, 575.
16. Ibid, Waltke, 578.
17. Ibid, Sailhamer, 224-225.

SESSION 7

1. Ibid, Mathews.
2. Brand, Chad, England, Archie & Draper, Charles, Eds., "Definition of Goshen" *Holman Illustrated Bible Dictionary* (Nashville, TN: B&H Publishing Group, 2009). Retrieved from https://app.wordsearchbible.com, accessed on April 26, 2019.
3. Benson Commentary, "Genesis 45:10" Bible Hub, https://biblehub.com/commentaries/genesis/45-10.htm, accessed on April 26, 2019.
4. Ibid, Kidner, 222.
5. Ibid, Mathews.
6. Ibid.
7. Ibid.
8. Ibid, Waltke, 589.

9. Ibid, 590.
10. Ibid, Mathews.
11. Ibid

SESSION 8

1. "Primogeniture," *Bible Hub* https://biblehub.com/topical/p/primogeniture.htm, accessed on April 29, 2019.
2. Ibid, Swanson.
3. Ibid, Sailhamer, 233.
4. Ibid, Waltke, 608.
5. Ibid, Sailhamer, 235-236.
6. Ibid, Sailhamer, 235.
7. Victor Hamilton, *The New International Commentary: The Book of Genesis, Chapters 18–50* (Grand Rapids, MI: Eerdmans Publishing Company, 2010), 679. Retrieved from https://app.wordsearchbible.com, accessed on April 30, 2019.
8. Ibid, Mathews.
9. Ibid, Mathews.
10. Ibid, Waltke, 622.
11. Ibid, Sailhamer, 239.
12. Craig R. Koester, *The Anchor Bible Commentary: Hebrews, A New Translation with Introduction and Commentary* (New York, NY: Doubleday, 2001), 500.

NOTES

NOTES

NOTES

ADDITIONAL STUDIES
FROM KELLY MINTER

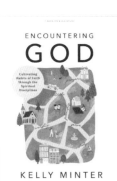

ENCOUNTERING GOD
Cultivating Habits of Faith Through the Spiritual Disciplines
7 sessions

Unpack the biblical foundation for spiritual disciplines, including ways to practice disciplines like prayer, study, worship, rest, simplicity, generosity, celebration, and more.

lifeway.com/encounteringgod

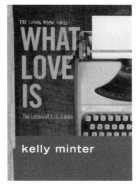

WHAT LOVE IS
The Letters of 1, 2, 3 John
7 sessions

Delve into the letters of 1, 2, and 3 John, written to encourage followers of Jesus to remain faithful to the truth. Glimpse not only the heart of John but also the heart of Jesus.

lifeway.com/whatloveis

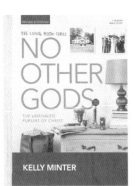

NO OTHER GODS
The Unrivaled Pursuit of Christ
8 sessions

Learn to identify the functional gods you may unknowingly be serving to experience the abundant life only Jesus can give.

lifeway.com/noothergods

NEHEMIAH
A Heart That Can Break
7 sessions

Nehemiah's heart was so broken for those in need that he left the comfort of his Persian palace to help them. Are you ready to let God break your heart for a hurting, lost world and move you to be the hands and feet of Jesus?

lifeway.com/nehemiah

RUTH
Loss, Love & Legacy
7 sessions

Walk through the book of Ruth and discover God's faithfulness in suffering, His immeasurable grace where we least expect it, and the way Ruth's story points toward Jesus.

lifeway.com/ruth

ALL THINGS NEW
A Study on 2 Corinthians
8 sessions

Study the letter of 2 Corinthians to discover how God can use you no matter your situation.

lifeway.com/allthingsnew

lifeway.com/kellyminter
800.458.2772

Lifeway women

Will you join Kelly
IN CARING FOR THE POOR, THE ORPHANED & THE FORGOTTEN?

Justice & Mercy International (JMI) is a Christ-centered, non-profit organization that cares for the vulnerable and forgotten in the Amazon and Moldova. Join Kelly, our long-time mission partner, in making a difference with JMI. **Scan the QR code** below or visit *justiceandmercy.org/cultivate* for more information.

Connect WITH JMI

Follow us on social media to keep up with the work of JMI.

  @JusticeAndMercyInt   @JusticeMercyInt

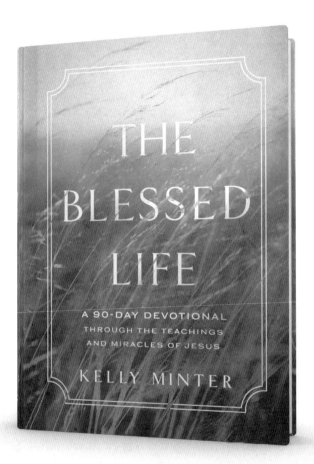

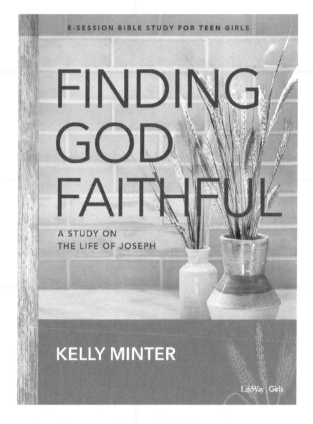

Get the most from your study.

COMPANION
PRODUCTS

DVD set, includes 8 video teaching sessions from Kelly Minter, each approximately 35 minutes

eBook with video access, includes 8 video teaching sessions from Kelly Minter, each approximately 35 minutes

IN THIS STUDY, YOU'LL:

- Place your hope in the God who is with you
- Learn to trust God's purposes when life doesn't make sense
- Recognize how God is working in your waiting
- Rest in the sufficiency of God's presence in every circumstance

To enrich your study experience, consider the accompanying *Finding God Faithful* video teaching sessions, approximately 35 minutes, from Kelly Minter.

STUDYING ON YOUR OWN?

Watch Kelly Minter's teaching sessions, available via redemption code for individual video-streaming access, printed in this Bible study book.

LEADING A GROUP?

Each group member will need a *Finding God Faithful* Bible study book, which includes video access. Because all participants will have access to the video content, you can choose to watch the videos outside of your group meeting if desired. Or, if you're watching together and someone misses a group meeting, they'll have the flexibility to catch up! A DVD set is also available to purchase separately if desired.

Browse companion products, a free session sample, video clips, church promotional materials, and more at

lifeway.com/findinggodfaithful